*This is a beautiful book; a ge[...]
insights. Through his own per[...]
the Middle East, Shadi helps*
*Lord's unfolding plans to bring complete [...]
only to Israel, but to all of her neighbours as well.*
**Joel Richardson, New York Times bestselling author,
filmmaker and speaker**

*As a profound and thought-provoking study of the Bible,
Shadi presents the role of Egypt and Iran in the history of
the Jewish nation and pointing to their continued role in
Israel's future. Shadi's deep understanding of the Bible,
his commitment to the Lord and his love for the nations
shines through his writing.
This is a "must read" for anyone interested in the past
and future of Egypt, Iran, or Israel.*
**Dr. Hormoz, Shariat Founder of Iran Alive,
author and pastor**

*The story of Abraham's family is at the epicentre of the
Christian faith; it is the stage set to display God's glory to
the whole earth. This book is a very timely resource in the
wake of the Isaiah 62 Fast (7-28 May 2023) in which
more than five million believers prayed for Israel. Shadi
shares his personal journey into partnership with God
related to the biblical narrative of Israel, Egypt, Iran and
other countries in the Middle East. His journey is the
result of prayerfully poring over Scripture for decades.
Shadi's life and writing inspires, provokes and equips
readers to reach to know God's heart and to partner
deeply with Him in His glorious end-time purposes.*
**Mike Bickle, International House of
Prayer of Kansas City**

ISRAEL

BORN IN

EGYPT

RAISED IN

IRAN

REDISCOVERING ANCIENT ROOTS

Dedication

This book is dedicated to the Egyptian and Persian martyrs who gave their lives over the centuries for the love of Jesus.

To the great cloud of witnesses; to all those who did not love their lives even unto death, whose souls are before the Altar of the Lord even now crying out, "How long, oh Lord!" (Revelation 6:9,10)

To the Jewish people who have passed down the faith to us today.

To my late father, who was a writer and the best storyteller; you've always blessed and supported what God was doing in my life. Even when I chose to let go of my medical career, you released me to go to the nations. Now I am at another milestone by finishing this book...I wish you were still around to read it and to celebrate with me. I miss you!

Acknowledgements

It is finished! I can finally say that I have done it—I've written my first book. For many years I planned to write this book, started and stopped, and kept going through this never-ending cycle until I attended a coaching class by Matt Bird. Within six months, my book was finished. Matt's coaching and ability to convince me that I could write and that my writing would be unique and inspiring paid off. Matt, thank you!

My goal for the book was to keep it simple enough for a child to understand and deep enough for seasoned adults to appreciate. My children helped me keep that balance. I loved watching their fascination and giggles as they read some parts about them in the book. I loved getting their comments and questions, also their edits were very helpful. If it doesn't make sense to a child, then it's too complicated! Thank you guys; love you tons!

My wife is my hero. She never ceases to amaze me with her hidden skills. She worked overtime, proofreading, editing, connecting the dots in many places where it only made sense to me. This book is now excellent because of you. I could not have done it without you. Thank you, Habibi!

I want to thank my local community for your patience and support while I took extra time away to focus on this project!

Jackie, though you were very busy with your own PHD, you offered to help with the first round of edits. Your comments and insights were extremely helpful, keeping me organised and to the point.

Daniel, your constant support and mentoring over the years helped shape the man I am today. Thank you for going on this book-writing journey with me.

Bedros, your friendship to me and your family's to ours has deeply enriched our lives. It was your idea to join Matt's writing course together and your enthusiasm about this book and cheerleading kept me going. Thank you!

Finally, I want to give all the thanks and honour to my teacher and helper, the one who gave me understanding and inspiration for the content of this book: the Holy Spirit. Your constant reminders of what scriptures to use and stories to tell made writing this book a fascinating daily encounter with you. From the bottom of my heart, I say "Thank you, Lord!"

Contents

ISRAEL, BORN IN EGYPT, RAISED IN IRAN

SHADI

Foreword

Rick Ridings, Asher Intrater and David Demian

(Editorial Note: Rarely does a book contain a foreword written by three authors; however, the uniqueness of their combined perspectives on this theme created a beautiful reflection of the heart of this book that we felt important to share.)

It is an honour to recommend not only this book, but the author to you. After having lived and ministered for a quarter of a century across the Middle East, I have found that those living in a particular nation often carry a very deep understanding of the Scriptures concerning that nation. However, there can be a type of nearsightedness that comes with such a depth of scope. Shadi offers deep and unique insights that help us to know the Lord's heart for Egypt and Iran, while maintaining clarity about the unique calling upon Israel as the First-Born nation.

I have known Shadi for about twenty years and this book reflects his steady, unwavering pursuit of the Lord and his desire to truly know the heart of God. As he shares in his journey, it was his intense love for the Lord that led him to find God's heart, not only for one nation, but this love actually overcame nationalistic and religious prejudices, enabling him to receive the Lord's purposes for Israel, Egypt, Iran and the whole region.

Reading through the pages of this book ministered to me. I was personally touched by Shadi's deep trust in the Lord's ability to weave together the callings upon individuals, families and nations, even in the face of very real tensions. In sharing his own journey, Shadi shows us how overcoming trials in our own lives and families equips us to prepare the way of the Lord, in the Middle East and in our own nations.

I recommend this book because it is not an echo of others, but a voice formed by the Lord. It is a first-hand revelation that is the result of faithful seeking the Lord over decades. I was both blessed and challenged by many profound insights and I know you will be too.

Rick Ridings, Founder of Succat Hallel (24/7 house of prayer overlooking the Temple Mount in Jerusalem), Author (with his wife Patricia) of 'Shifting Nations through Houses of Prayer'

Shadi's new book is a rare combination of a biblical meditation, a scriptural text study and a personal journey. The perspective he has from Egypt, Iran and the prophetic prayer movement is truly unique.

As a Jewish spiritual brother, it is a joy to see this kind of writing come forward. This is a contribution to our continuing journey as Messianic Jews and Arab Christians throughout the Middle East. It is part of restoring ancient family covenants going back to Abraham, which form the foundation of the history of the church, Israel and the nations.

In fact, the roots of the relationship between Egypt, Israel and Iran go all the way back to God's purposes for a global family in the Garden of Eden. There, God made a perfect world. He gave that world to the first man and woman: Adam and Eve. He told them to multiply. There you have it: a global family in a global Garden of Eden—that is the plan.

Because of sin and rebellion, that plan was disrupted. But God has not given up. He is continuing with His original intention through a long and patient process of calling human beings back to Himself. God's covenant with Adam was continued through Noah and then through Abraham.

We see a principle emerge during the stay of Abraham's descendants in Egypt, which was then the greatest Empire of the world. When Joseph ruled as prime minister, both the Egyptians and the Israelites were blessed. The Pharaoh was benevolent and there was peace, prosperity and righteousness, as well as a loving relationship between the Israelites and the Egyptians (note Genesis 50:7-11). That was God's plan for Egypt and Israel: mutual blessing. That was His original intention, and it remains so today.

That purpose was disrupted by sin. The next Pharaoh was evil; the Israelites were enslaved and abused. Finally, Egypt was judged and punished at the Exodus, in the time of Moses. The Empire of Egypt was diminished. Gradually, a new Empire grew up in Canaan, conquered by the Israelites. This Israelite Empire became the strongest in the world at the time of David and Solomon. Solomon's Empire included a covenant with Lebanon, Egypt and the Transjordan area. (I Kings 3:1, 5:1) There was peace and prosperity; the Jews and Arabs lived together in harmony; the greater Abrahamic family of nations was growing.

Israel then sinned and was punished by God. God sent the prophet Jonah to Assyria (Nineveh). After the great revival there, the nation of Assyria grew to become the strongest Empire in the world. They conquered and exiled the northern tribes of Israel. (Jonah 3, Isaiah 10, II Kings 17)

After Assyria, Babel (Iraq) grew strong. When Israel rebelled, God used the Iraqi Empire to destroy and exile Judah. At the height of their Empire, under King Nebuchadnezzar, the prophet Daniel served as the prime minister. (see Daniel 2:48-49) We see here another glimpse of the right, covenantal alignment of the Abrahamic family of nations. But then Iraq also sinned. The next nation to arise was Persia (Iran). At the height of their power, Mordecai served as the prime minister . (Esther 10:2-3) Again, the same divine pattern of mutual blessing was repeated.

The history of the Tanakh (Old Testament) period ends with Persia financing and supporting the rebuilding of the Temple in Jerusalem and thus supporting the restoration of the nation of Israel itself. (II Chronicles 36, Ezra 1)

Centuries later, we see in that very temple descendants of Egypt, Mesopotamia, Arabia and others present at the time of the outpouring of the Holy Spirit on the day of Pentecost (feast of Shavuot) in Acts 2 (note verses 5-11). Amazingly, the remnant of the nations from the extended family of Abraham were present at the first day of the start of the community of faith in Jerusalem. Thus, we see that the international ekklesia is the spiritual extension of God's covenant with Abraham and the people of Israel.

Certainly, most of the history of the Middle East has been one of war and enmity. However, amid those struggles we can see the thread of God's eternal purpose for good. The highway that Abraham walked from Ur of the Chaldees to Israel, down to Egypt and back again is being rebuilt today by the loving relationships of all the spiritual sons and daughters of Abraham.

Shadi's life and this book express his journey on this ancient highway of divine covenant and mutual blessing. The family of faith is being restored.

Asher Intrater, President, Tikkun Global, Jerusalem

It has been a joy and pleasure to know Shadi and his wife and their lovely children. In the past ten years or so, this family has won the hearts of the Watchmen global family of nations, with the pure perfume of their worship, rising as a sweet incense to the Lord. Shadi is a dear friend, not only because we share a similar journey of being medical doctors before we were called into full-time service to the Lord, but more so because we share the same heart for the Lord. Shadi's life is a testimony to all that the Lord is doing in the Middle East and in the nations beyond. His deep friendship with God is inspiring.

This is a book for those who desire to experience the heart of Father God for His global family of nations, particularly in the Middle East. To my knowledge, few in the Kingdom Family have been able to write about the prophetic significance of the Isaiah 19 nations with the same clarity, humility and sensitivity to the Holy Spirit as Shadi has in this book.

The Lord promises us in Amos 3:7: "Surely the Lord God does nothing unless He reveals His secret plan to His servants the prophets." I believe He is seeking sons and daughters who are inclining their ears, quieting down to hear, intimate friends in whom He can confide His counsel for these critical times. This book bears the fruit of a man who lives the life of closely obeying and passionately following the Heart of the Lord. As such, he writes with spiritual authority and brings heavenly perspective to what the world views as complex and contentious.

What would it take for the Isaiah 19 nations to become a blessing to all the nations on earth? When would the presence of the Lord be pleased to dwell in the heart of His body, where all His sons and daughters manifest His love, revealing Messiah to the world? Can there be oneness among the sons of Ishmael and the sons of Isaac?

No human government has yet been able to successfully secure lasting peace in the Middle East. The Lord of Hosts is the only one, true and eternal solution. The Lord has promised us in Isaiah 19 that the day of fulfilment will come. His face will shine with His glory on all who are yielded to our Father's heart, willing to choose to live in oneness with His presence and with each other. We will yearn to join in faith and spirit, the Family of God from every nation turning toward our Father, ready to hear and be the answer to His heart's cry.

No matter how long or how terrible the pain and suffering against the seed of Messiah, or the seed of Abraham, we know the end of the story. Life will prevail. The risen Lord overcomes. The Lord of hosts has promised that though He strikes, He will heal. He will answer every nation's heart cry for Him, but will we hear and respond to the cry of His heart? This book is an invitation.

David Demian, Director, Watchmen for the Nations

SHADI

Preface

Many people are disconnected from what is happening in the Middle East today. Those who are paying attention often do so with predisposed sentiments toward one "side" of the story. General negativity is often implicated in light of numerous atrocities that have taken place in the region over centuries. People who have personal ties to the region may naturally have a negative generalisation of nations or ethnic groups for any historic injustice, especially if it was perpetrated against ancestors, immediate family or friends.

For those who embrace a biblical worldview of God's redemptive plan for all nations, it can still be difficult to navigate historical, ethnic and personal biases. Though one may have a genuine desire to be true to God's heart for all nations, when it comes to the issue of Israel and the Jewish people, most feel compelled to choose sides: either the side of Israel or the side of ethnic groups from the surrounding nations. [1] If one stands with God's purposes for Israel, the temptation is to reject, or at least forget about, His purposes for the surrounding nations. If one empathises towards the side of the Arab nations, the danger is to completely reject and oppose God's purposes for Israel. This tension is real, especially when it is inundated with political perspectives.

Most don't recognise that they have a negative predisposition until it is triggered by a situation, a conversation or perhaps even by the nudges of the Holy Spirit. In our genuine desire to agree with God, we must ask Him to shine the light of revelation on our hearts to show us our blind spots through the truth of His word.

I remember years ago, in a corporate prayer meeting, a lady came to me after I had prayed for "the Church in Egypt", sharing that she had always hated Egypt because of how they treated the Jewish people in captivity before the Exodus. "After you prayed," she said, "I feel like I started to see a different side of the big picture."

Up to that moment, she was carrying a three-thousand-year-old offence in her heart. There was a need for the power of revelation, by which the Holy Spirit could "break" this mindset and help her to see the Egyptian people today through God's eyes and not only to see them through a historical lens of the past. Interestingly enough, years later, the Lord called this woman to work and minister in Egypt!

In another context, a man shared a similar life-changing experience. He was passively listening to an online prayer meeting and noticed a language he'd never heard before... the Holy Spirit drew his attention. As he listened intently, he realised that they were praying and singing in Farsi (the language of Iran). He fell on his knees and began to weep, feeling the intense love of God for the Iranian people. He said that he had always been an "advocate" and "intercessor" for Israel, but never considered praying for the nations that are the "enemies" of Israel. But in a moment, the Holy Spirit gave him a new perspective and his heart was enlarged to no longer see the people of the nations that surround Israel as enemies, but to love them as Jesus loves them.

Both individuals grew up in western contexts. For many who are living in the Middle East, the negative sentiment is directed toward Israel. For Christians born and raised in the region, the Bible is taught through the lens of a theological opinion called Replacement Theology, which, in a simplistic explanation, means that the Church has replaced Israel. It follows, therefore, that there is no distinctive place for the nation and the ethnic people of Israel in God's redemptive plans.

Years ago, a young man from Egypt was at one of our conferences. He was very vocal about his negative sentiments against Israel, as he had noticed several who were zealous about Israel. Suddenly, in the middle of a time of worship, he started weeping and crying out loud with his hands shaking and sweating. He was in what some would call spiritual travail, something he had never experienced before. After this encounter, he came to me, very confused about what had happened. He said, "As I felt a burning sensation over my body, I kept hearing the voice of the Lord saying, 'I love Israel, I love Israel.'" He didn't know what to do with this.

The next day, he was in prayer with his Bible open, processing this with the Lord. Everywhere he turned, he suddenly saw passages speaking of God's heart for Israel. He began to realise that God still loves the Jewish people and He still has a distinct plan for them. This transformative experience was the work of the Holy Spirit and demonstrates the power of the Word of God, which can literally break chains of prejudice and hatred in the mind.

Regardless of which of these two camps you may be in, as you read this book you may find that you are on the *wrong side*. Yes, I'm talking to you!

When Joshua met the Angel of the Lord, he desperately asked, "Are you for us, or for our enemies? Are you with us or with them?" The Lord's answer was quick and sharp: "*Neither*. I am the commander of the Lord's army."

He was saying, "I am not here to serve your agenda, I have my own agenda. The question I now ask you is this: Are you on my side? Are you aligned with my heart? Are you willing to do whatever I ask you to do?" (Joshua 5:13,14)

Perhaps God is not on one side or the other. Perhaps we all need to answer the question God asked Joshua: are we on the side of the Lord? We may need to put on a different lens to see the issues more clearly. I hope that through the stories and journey this book lays out, we will begin to see through God's eyes.

We are seeing global shifts and shakings occur with an increasing frequency: the rapid devastation of entire nations (Syria, Iraq and Ukraine/Russian War); refugee crises in Europe; the global lockdown of 2020 and an increase in significant earthquakes. Crises will only continue to escalate in all the world, but particularly in the region of the Middle East, where Jesus is coming back. Having the correct biblical understanding will position the Church to stand on the side of the Lord when pressure is most extreme.

In the Second World War, most of the German people were deceived by political and religious propaganda and complied with the "the wrong side" resulting in the betrayal of the entire Jewish people and the massacre of millions. We are coming to a time when the church will need to take a stand, not for or against a people, but for the Lord, His truth and His ways. We can't afford to be uninformed, unprepared and disconnected, leaving our sentimentality vulnerable to manipulation and consequently forming wrong alliances.

It is with this in mind that I have written this book. As a man born and raised in the Middle East, I have been on a journey of seeking to know God and His purposes, not only for my nation of origin, but for all the nations.

As the Lord began to help me understand His heart and purposes for Israel, He also showed me that His heart has always been to include the nations in His redemptive plan. Two main nations that have consistently been used by God to escort Israel into her identity and destiny are the nations of Egypt and what was ancient Persia (now modern-day Iran). This book highlights how the calling of these two nations is intricately connected to the calling of Israel. Together, these three nations will stand as "a blessing in the midst of the land" with the other surrounding nations, as declared in Isaiah 19.[2]

I have structured the book into four sections. Though this book is not primarily about the specific message of Isaiah 19, an overarching theme of this important passage is highlighted throughout the book. So, it will be helpful to read the book in the order of the sections and chapters, as their sequence lays out a continuous storyline. Each chapter highlights not only historical biblical characters and truths, but also spiritual lessons that we can all grow in today.

There is another overarching theme of wells woven into the book. Wells were essential to the survival of the communities in the ancient world. In Scripture, we see wells not only as a source of physical sustenance, but a place where God meets with His people and, often, marks or even alters the course of their lives. In our context, we will highlight few of these literal/physical wells that show key moments in the journey of God's people, in and out of Egypt and Iran. Jeremiah had declared to Israel that she, desperate with thirst, had dug wells that produced no water, having forgotten that God alone is the only source of water that would satisfy her. (Jeremiah 2:13). God meets with His people around wells to remind them He is the source of their existence and sustenance.[3]

There are four goals I hope this book can serve to advance.

Firstly, to offer what I have come to understand of the role of Egypt and Iran in God's redemptive plan, not only for the Jewish people but for all nations.

Secondly, to broaden perspectives; to highlight that God's choice of Israel as His first born is about having a family from the nations. God chose Israel so that Israel can bring His glory to the nations. The nations have always been His intention.

Thirdly, to challenge you to open your mind and heart to embrace all the nations of the Middle East and to inspire and equip you to pray for the church in this region and for the salvation of Israel.

Lastly, to facilitate conversations with the Lord; I pray that the Holy Spirit would encounter you, escort you to deeper truths in your walk with Jesus and, perhaps, stir you—for a season or a lifetime—to partner with His purposes in these nations.

In the Book of Daniel, an angel spoke about a generation to come; his words may be more relevant to us today than ever before:

"But you, Daniel, shut up the words and seal the book until the time of the end, many shall run to and fro and knowledge shall increase ... Many shall be purified, made white and refined but the wicked shall do wickedly and none of the wicked shall understand, but the wise shall understand." (Daniel 12:4,9,10)

There is a need in this generation to walk in understanding and to instruct many. We need the help of the Holy Spirit to teach us His word, His ways and His plans so that we would know how to stand in this season of human history.

This is my prayer for you:

"That you may be filled with the knowledge of His will in all wisdom and spiritual understanding, that you may walk worthy of the Lord, fully pleasing him in every good work." (Colossians 1:9,10)

As you read through this book, I would ask you to pray this over your own heart. May Jesus unlock treasures from His word and deposit them directly in your heart producing eternal fruit.

Map of Egypt, Assyria, Israel, c. 670 B.C.[4]

Section 1 -
Laying Foundations

" Blessed be Egypt my people, Assyria my handiwork, and Israel my inheritance."

(Isaiah 19:25)

The origins of human history lie in what is referred to as the Fertile Crescent. This area is rich with historical, anthropological, cultural and religious keys. The story of Israel is right in the centre. As is the way of life within that region, the journey of Israel is nomadic; yet there are two clear bookends in terms of geography and historical influence: Egypt to the West and, to the East, the area that includes borders of modern-day Iran. In the following chapters, I lay a foundation for the reasons behind our focus on these three nations: Egypt, Iran and Israel. The first step is to begin at ground zero of how we personally and individually come to this topic. Then, we zoom out to the starting point of the family storyline.

Why is Israel—the land and the people—important and relevant to us today? One simple reason is that it is eternally important and relevant to Him.

Chapter 1

Barriers - A Personal Journey

We all cherish the memories of the places we grew up: the streets, the sounds, the food and the people. When we tell our story, we have a deep sense of longing for those places and moments. Whenever we go back to visit, it invokes in us a sense of joy and wholeness.

The first time I visited Israel, I was overwhelmed by a phrase I heard the Holy Spirit speak to me. As I walked around the cities, visiting the sights, the Holy Spirit spoke clearly to me, saying, "Welcome to my home." Immediately, I was filled with awe mixed with sorrow. Awe, because I realised that I was standing on holy ground, a place where His holy feet once walked and where His holy blood was shed for me. With sorrow, because I realised that I had never thought to cherish the streets that fill His memories, the streets where the events of His life occurred. It was the first time I realised that the events we read as a historical record in the Bible are as alive in His heart today as they were back then. He still remembers them! It is personal to Him where He was born, where He grew up and where His eternal blood was shed. It is where He will return one more time, restoring all things.

Why is Israel—the land and the people—important and relevant to us today? One simple reason is that it is eternally important and relevant to Him. Therefore, it should be important and relevant to me as his friend, as his disciple. But, like many in the Middle East, I had barriers in my heart and mind that blocked me from not only recognising that He cares about this land and people, but also from being able to love, bless and pray for the people and the land of Israel.

Painful memories

For some, the issue of Israel triggers real pain and real loss. Many have lost loved ones in wars between Israel and the surrounding nations. Many have lost homes, land and livelihoods and face a scary, uncertain future. Undoubtedly, the loss is on both sides, but because Israel, (as it stands today) is often perceived to have received a better deal, Arabs (Muslim and Christian) who have suffered real loss find it incredibly difficult to forgive, love or bless. All that is there is pain and resentment.

Geopolitical

Most Christians and Muslims living in the Middle East will live and die without ever meeting one Jewish person, despite the geographical proximity of Israel to the surrounding nations. Crossing that border causes many challenges before, during and after the visit. Most of the surrounding governments don't allow their people to visit Israel, except under certain circumstances. The visas are difficult to obtain. If you end up receiving permission to travel, then security and surveillance issues are to be expected during the visit and for a long time after returning home. Therefore, most people just avoid this hassle altogether and don't even consider a visit. [4]

Social

Most people In the Middle East consider the Jews to be the deserving recipients of God's wrath. In Arabic, the term "Jew" is derogatory, mostly used to demean others. This is both seed and fruit of Islamic theology. It was my experience, growing up as an Arab Christian in a Muslim-majority society that, over the years, the same negative sentiments were fostered in my own heart and mind. I remember hearing the call to prayer on Fridays followed by long declarations and prayers asking God to destroy the Jews. Of course, at a human and moral level, I totally disagreed with what I heard. Nevertheless, I can see how these sentiments were unconsciously internalised, creating walls and prejudices within my mind and soul.

Spiritual

Most feuds (ethnic, economic, national, etc.) go back to a historic conflict. There's a deep spiritual wound in the hearts of both Arabs and Jews that goes all the way back to the conflict between Isaac and Ishmael, Sarah and Hagar, Jacob and Esau[5]. This wound is more than historic, I believe it is spiritual.[6]

Theological

I have touched on the barrier within Islamic theology. As for the barrier within Christian theology, most Bible teachers in the Middle East teach that the Church has totally replaced Israel. This view is known as

Supersessionism, or Replacement Theology. According to this view, it follows that there is no special place or calling that still exists on Israel and that the promise of the land given to Abraham and his descendants has become obsolete because the Church is now the heir of Christ. [7]

My Barriers Broken

I did not realise that I had some of these barriers in my own heart until after I moved to the United States to intern with an international ministry. It quickly became obvious to me that this ministry valued, prayed for and honoured the Jewish people in a distinct way. There was a whole room designated to pray for Israel! I was offended. "Oh great! Here we go," I thought to myself, "God, have you tricked me by bringing me here?!"[8] It didn't take long for me to be challenged by what seemed to me as exaggerated attention toward and affection for Israel and the Jews. It irritated me when I heard people pray for Israel, when I saw them holding flags and dancing in "Hebrew" style. The offence was constant; anger was growing. That's when I knew, in my heart, that something was wrong, but I did not know the way forward.

I particularly remember when during an all-night prayer meeting, I was asking the Lord to show me His purpose for my life. Throughout the night, one prayer lingered in my heart: "Lord, what is your purpose for my life?" At the time, I was a medical doctor and had been feeling a tug on my heart to step into full-time ministry, giving up my medical career. I was in a deep wrestle. I needed understanding about what the next step in my life was going to be, what it would be like. I was growing impatient. "Lord, what is your purpose for my life?" I asked persistently, without receiving any clear answers.

Suddenly, one of the leaders came to the platform announcing that he would be praying for Israel. "Oh, not again, please," I thought, "I am in a deep place with the Lord contending for His purpose for my life. Give me a break!" The next sentence that came out of his mouth was like an arrow that deeply pierced my heart. He said, "God's purpose is Israel." As soon as he made the statement, God said to me, "This is the answer to the question that you've been asking me tonight. My purpose is Israel." I could not stop weeping as I felt the weight of the truth that was being declared in my spirit. I recognised that my destiny in God, whether I liked it or not, was intertwined with God's plan for Israel. Until I allowed him to remove this barrier, which was ultimately keeping me from a part of His heart, I would remain stuck. I was humbled. I said yes in my spirit to this truth, longing to be reconciled to this purpose in the Lord's heart, but I still felt bound in my mind and soul. Reconciling took time.

On another occasion, I was in a meeting with some Messianic Jews [9]. One of them invited the 'Arab Brothers' to come to the front and stand under a chuppah they had set up. If you are like I was, you are probably wondering what on earth a chuppah is! It is a canopy used in Jewish weddings and represents coming under the shelter of God.

When I heard this invitation, I resisted it with everything within. "Thank you, but no thank you. I am not interested in Christianity shows." I told myself that I could receive from my seat. But the persistent nudge from the Holy Spirit wouldn't let me off the hook. I knew I should get up and stand with these brothers. I had to swallow my Arab pride and obey the Holy Spirit. So, I did; but it was totally out of my comfort zone. As I closed my eyes, almost immediately I heard the voice of the Father so clearly in my spirit saying, "Welcome to the family of Abraham. You've come under the shelter of the God of Abraham, Isaac and Jacob." I started weeping as I realised that my Christian faith is rooted in the Jewish family tree. As a Christian, I am grafted into that tree and my faith started way before I personally said yes to Jesus. It started when Abraham said yes to Yahweh to be a father of many nations!

In that moment, I realised that my faith is an extension of the faith of Abraham. As I stood under the chuppah, tears flowed down my face as I felt that I was now home and that I belonged to a much bigger family than I had realised.

Those experiences were catalytic, propelling me to search out the scriptures, asking for revelation and understanding. One day, as I was reading Isaiah 60, my eyes were opened. "Oh my gosh, it's talking about Zion as a real geographical place in Israel!" In a moment, the veil was removed and I could see the Scriptures for what they really meant, without the theological filters with which I had been raised.

After years of further study, Scripture has continued to emphasise the truth that God is not done with Israel. This book is a product of thousands of hours of prayer, meditation, study and wrestling with the Lord over these truths. In that journey, what my mind struggled to accept and believe, like arrows striking my heart, the Holy Spirit brought greater light and conviction. I pray that the pages of this book will usher you into a new realm of revelation and understanding that will bring you to a deeper relationship with our Lord.

*He is "the Holy One of Israel"—
that is not only a description, but
also one of His names!*

Chapter 2

The Family Table

I have six young children. One of the best moments for me as a father is when we sit around the dinner table enjoying a good meal and sharing time together. I love to see the different ways each of my children express themselves, talking about their day and sharing their experiences. On the other hand, it can be a very disturbing experience when everyone is talking over each other, fighting over who gets the biggest piece of garlic bread or largest scoop of ice cream.

One of the main things that trigger strife and jealousy between siblings is comparing the gifts that each one receives from the parent. Imagine that a child receives a scoop of chocolate ice cream and the other sibling receives a piece of chocolate cake. These two children may get sidetracked by feeling wronged that they each received a different gift. They may perceive the parent as "unfair" because he didn't give them each the same treat. Perhaps, even to an outsider looking in, this might seem inequitable.

God is a father and longs for all His children to come together in love and harmony. This sense of harmony comes first and foremost from an absolute confidence in the father and his love; a confidence in knowing that he is good and that he desires to give the best to each of his children. We know that God gives perfect gifts to each child according to His generous heart, His perfect leadership and the richness of His wisdom. (James 1:17)

Each gift is given for the greater benefit of the whole family—it is not primarily for the individual. Though the gifts given may be different, the goal for each is the same: that each member of the family, using their unique gifts, would serve the entirety of the family so that together they would walk in fullness of their identity. [10]So the Father's desire is that as His child, one would trust that whether they get chocolate ice cream or chocolate cake, it is a gift to be enjoyed and shared!

The Gift to Israel

When it comes to Israel and God's choosing this people over the rest of the nations to be his "firstborn" (Exodus 4:22), we may have feelings like the child given a different treat. We may be asking ourselves similar questions: Why were they given a special place? What was so special about Isaac and why was he chosen over Ishmael? Why did God give them a "promised" land? What about the other nations? What about my nation? Doesn't God love all people equally?

Why is Israel a chosen nation, and for what purpose are they chosen? Let's take a moment and look at a few scriptures that will help us answer this.

"For you are a holy people to the Lord your God; the Lord your God has chosen you to be a people for Himself, a special treasure above all the peoples on the face of the earth. The Lord did not set His love on you, nor choose you because you were more in number than any other people, for you were the least of all peoples; but because the Lord loves you, and because He would keep the oath which He swore to your fathers." (Deuteronomy 7:6-9)

According to the above passage, the simple answer is that they are chosen because God chose them and He chose them for Himself. God initiated a covenant that He is faithful to keep; He is committed to love for He is love. God has the right to choose—after all, He is God. If His choices offend us, we should consider that because we are not God, we may need to seek understanding and let go of our ignorance and offence that could keep us in unbelief. We must humbly acknowledge our need for Him to lead our hearts to know His affections and zeal, His wisdom and purpose in each choice He has made.

Not only did God choose and consecrate Israel for Himself as a holy people, but He went further: He chose to bind His own identity and His name to them forever. He is "the Holy One of Israel"— that is not only a description, but also one of His names!

"But now, thus says the Lord, who created you, O Jacob. And He who formed you, O Israel: Fear not, for I have redeemed you; I have called you by your name; You are Mine ... For I am the Lord your God, The Holy One of Israel, your Saviour... I am the Lord, your Holy One, The Creator of Israel, your King." (Isaiah 43:1,3,15)

Israel and the Gentile nations

As we trace Israel's history, the journey of her formation in and out of different nations, we discover the intention in God's heart. God gave Israel the covenants, the law, the prophets and the priesthood, calling them to reflect who

He is and to represent Him to the nations. Their way of life and their heart posture was supposed to reveal who God is, so that all nations would come to the knowledge of God and be saved. (Isaiah 45:22,23) The greatest gift He gave to the nations was Himself, that He would be known through the witness of His chosen people.

Unfortunately, the nation could not walk this out successfully for extended periods of time, but with His grace, many individuals did. Solomon's wisdom was sought after by the nations. Joseph's understanding saved the world. Daniel's faith and prophetic insight shifted history, and the list goes on.

Even when God disciplined Israel by sending them to Babylon, He was not only dealing with their disobedience, but He was also providing a means of redemption to Babylon. God could have disciplined Israel in her homeland, but in sending Israel to another nation, He allowed that nation to then experience the God of heaven through the testimony of faithful witnesses amid their captivity.

Paul takes this concept further in Romans 11, indicating the wisdom of God, even in using Israel's malady and hard heart to bring salvation for the Gentiles and, in turn, setting the stage for her own turning back to the Lord.

"For I do not desire, brethren, that you should be ignorant of this mystery, lest you should be wise in your own opinion, that blindness in part has happened to Israel until the fullness of the Gentiles has come in. And so, all Israel will be saved ... Concerning the gospel they are enemies for your sake, but concerning the election they are beloved for the sake of the fathers. For the gifts and the calling of God are irrevocable ... For God has committed them all to disobedience, that He might have mercy on all. Oh, the depth of the riches of both the wisdom and knowledge of God! How unsearchable are His judgments and His ways past finding out!" (Romans 11:25-36)

Between Egypt and Persia

Two primary nations that have been positioned by God to shape Israel's history, identity and destiny are the nations of Egypt and Iran. The stories of these three nations are deeply intertwined. Not only are they significant in the Old Testament, but also at the birth of the Messiah, Pentecost and in context to the Second-Coming.

1 - Historical Bookends

The story of Israel in the Old Testament begins in Egypt and ends in Iran. Israel was birthed in Egypt and four hundred years later, they inherit the promised land of Canaan. But due to their rebellion, they lose their freedom and end up in captivity in Assyria, Babylon and then Persia. At the end of seventy years of exile, they were allowed to leave Persia to return to their homeland and rebuild their nation.

The book of Genesis closes with Israel in Egypt and the birth of the nation. The books of Daniel, Ezra, Nehemiah, Esther, Haggai, Zechariah and Malachi were written during the Persian era marking the end of the Old Testament. Israel was born in Egypt, raised and restored in Iran!

2 - Geographical Boundaries

In pursuit of God's calling, Abraham left his home in Ur of Chaldea (modern-day Iraq) and went down to Egypt, passing through Canaan on the way, where he later returned. It is within this geographical area that Abraham was promised a land "from the Nile to the Euphrates." (Genesis 15:18)

Isaiah 19, written more than a millennium after Abraham's lifetime, paints a beautiful picture that he is seeing at the end of the age, which realises the path of Abraham's footsteps.

"In that day there will be a highway from Egypt to Assyria. The Assyrians will go to Egypt and the Egyptians to Assyria. The Egyptians and Assyrians will worship together. In that day Israel will be the third, along with Egypt and Assyria, a blessing on the earth." (Isaiah 19:23-24 NIV)

Isaiah's prophecy is bringing together Abraham's descendants to the land that he was promised. Positioned at geographical ends of this highway, Egypt and Iran are, by divine design, called to be a blessing to Israel; together, becoming a blessing to the earth.

3 - Economic Ties

Two of Israel's sanctuaries of worship were built using Egyptian and Persian gold. At the time of the Exodus, Israel left with quite a collection of gold from the Egyptians. (Exodus 12:35,36) The Tabernacle of Moses was the first corporate sanctuary commissioned for the people of Israel. All the holy articles in it, including the Ark of the Covenant, were made using Egyptian gold. Centuries later, at the return from their exile, Cyrus, the king of Persia, financed, from his own treasury, the rebuilding of the city of Jerusalem and the temple. [11] He also gave back all the golden articles that were stolen from the temple during Israel's captivity seventy years before. After Cyrus, Darius continued this legacy of provision for the building of the temple. (Ezra 6:1-12) This was to be the very temple in which Jesus would stand centuries later, sharing the good news that His Father's House was a house of prayer for all nations! (Isaiah 56:7, Luke 19:46)

It is also interesting to see that this economic highway of provision between Egypt, Iran and Israel remained at the time of Jesus's birth. The Persian Magi gave gold to Jesus's family when they followed the star to worship Him as a young child. Fleeing as refugees to Egypt, the holy family was sustained by the gift of gold from Persia.[12]

4 - Biblical Significance

Next to Israel, Egypt is the most mentioned nation in the whole Bible. While Israel is referred to as "my people" throughout Scripture[13], it is interesting to note that Egypt is the only other nation in the Bible to be addressed as such: "Blessed be Egypt, my people." (Isaiah 19:25)

Another similarly shared reference (this time between Israel and Iran) is found in the writings of Jeremiah. Jeremiah 3:17 tells of a day when Israel will be called "the throne of the Lord". However, in Jeremiah 49:38, he also states, "I will set my throne in Elam." The area of Elam became part of the Persian Empire. There are also significant references in Scripture about Persia (some scholars count over two hundred references), the most notable containing the key events in the lives of some of the most famous of Biblical characters, Esther, Daniel and King Cyrus.

5 - Eschatological Significance

Even in the end of the age, these two nations will have a major role to play in events leading to the salvation of Israel and the return of Christ.

"It shall come to pass in that day that the Lord shall set his hand again the second time to recover the remnant of his people who are left from Assyria and Egypt, from Pathros and Cush, from Elam and Sinar from Hamath and the islands of the sea... there will be a highway for the remnant of his people who will be left from Assyria as it was for Israel in the day that he came up from the land of Egypt." (Isaiah 11:11)

"But it shall come to pass in the latter days, I will bring back the captives of Elam says the Lord." (Jeremiah 49:39)

These two passages suggest that at a future time, there will be a return of the Jewish people from these two lands (and more) as in the days of the Exodus.

Current Spiritual Battle and God's Answer

Today, Egypt is the centre of Sunni Islam and Iran is the centre of Shia Islam. These two main sects of Islam have fought against each other for centuries, but they have at least one thing in common: a goal to defeat and overtake the land of Israel and the city of Jerusalem for the cause of Islam.

On one end of the Isaiah 19 highway stands Iran, very vocal about its agenda to defeat, crush and eliminate their ideological enemies, the greatest of which is Israel. On the other end, standing in Cairo, Egypt, today is the oldest and the most strategic Islamic university that attracts thousands of students from all over the world and sends them back to their nations with not only skill and education, but with their ideology. I highlight these current dynamics to point out a spiritual battle behind the political and ideological conflicts in the region that is like a thorn in the side of the planet.

Knowing the current hostility between these three nations, it's hard to imagine how the breakthrough would come. Nonetheless, the Lord has uncovered the blueprints in Isaiah 19. He indicates that this miracle will be cultivated, perhaps even instigated, through worship. He will establish a canopy of worship all over this region, stretching it and establishing strong tent pegs at the corners of this area, so the whole earth would be blessed by the fragrance.[14]

Ethnicity is not what matters before God. What matters is that all who have been baptised by the same Spirit of God, which is what makes us sons and daughters of the Father and co-heirs with the Son, have become members of the same Family. (Romans 8:14-17)

Chapter 3

The Family Tree

*"For this reason, I kneel before the Father, from whom
every family in heaven and on earth derives its name."
(Ephesians 3:14,15)*

God desires a family. We trace this desire all the way back
to the moment of creation, as He created Adam and Eve
and enjoyed fellowship with them. In choosing to do
things their own way instead of God's, they lost spiritual
connection with Him and were cast out of the garden. In
His mercy, however, God gave them a promise of a seed
in their lineage that would restore everything back to
original design.

"I will put enmity between you and the woman, between
your seed and her seed; He shall bruise your head, and
you shall bruise His heel." (Genesis 3:15)

As we follow the Genesis account, we encounter God's
pain and sorrow over the condition of the earth. The
minds and hearts of humanity had been corrupted by evil,
except for one righteous man, Noah and his family. They
survived the flood and through them, the seed promised
to Eve is preserved. Generations pass and Abraham is
born. In his story, the seed is marked by a covenant. It
continues to be traced through the generations, until the
fullness of time had come when to a young virgin in Israel,
the foretold Messiah would be born, tracing His lineage
back to Abraham and Adam. (Luke 3:23-22) The entire
ancient history of the people of God in the Old Testament
climaxes at the coming of the Messiah, the Saviour of the

world. The choice of Israel as a people and later as a nation was a vehicle in and through which Christ Jesus would accomplish God's original plan to "crush the serpent's head" and restore humanity to Himself, bringing back the family of God and establishing His Kingdom on the earth.

A Family from the Nations

God is committed to having a family from every people, tribe and nation. In covenant partnership with Him, this global family (His Church, the Body of Christ, Jew and Gentile) is bringing His purposes to pass on earth as it is in heaven.

"After this I looked and there before me was a great multitude that no one could count, from every nation, tribe, people and language, standing before the throne and before the Lamb." (Revelation 7:9)

As was a common historical practice of many kingdoms, building national alliances through marriage, God loves to widen the reach of the roots and branches of "His" family tree by orchestrating beautiful cross-cultural marriages (mine is one of these). Let's take a look at some examples.

Abraham's Wives

Abraham, the Chaldean, had three wives. His first wife, Sarah (also Chaldean), though barren until the age of ninety, gave birth to the promised son, Isaac. His second wife, Hagar, was Egyptian and bore his first son Ishmael. His third wife, Keturah, bore him six children. (Genesis 25:1-4)

Ishmael (ethnically Egyptian and Chaldean) had twelve sons that became twelve tribes[15]. Abraham's second son, Isaac, was ethnically Chaldean (Chaldeans still inhabit modern day Iraq). Isaac had two sons, Jacob, who became the father of the twelve tribes of Israel; and Esau who became the father of tribes in modern-day Jordan[16]. The sons of Keturah were later sent to the East with gifts and eventually became the tribes that formed part of the region of ancient Assyria, parts of which include modern-day Saudi Arabia[17].

It is worth noting here that the people groups referenced in Isaiah 19 (Egypt, Israel and Assyria) trace their lineage back to Abraham's three wives: Hagar, Sarah and Keturah. More than a thousand years after Abraham, Isaiah was reaffirming God's people with the promise He made to Abraham, that there's a day coming when all His family will come together and all the nations of the earth will be blessed by it.

Joseph's Wife

In Egypt, Pharoah honoured Joseph by giving him an Egyptian wife (the daughter of a priest) and she bore two sons, Manasseh and Ephraim. Their mother tongue was Egyptian and they grew up educated by the customs and culture of Egypt. Joseph's two Egyptian sons later became two of the twelve tribes of Israel and received a land inheritance when Joshua led Israel into the Promised-Land.

Moses' Wife

Moses' wife, Zipporah, was the daughter of a Midianite priest; Midian was a son of Abraham through Keturah. (Genesis 25:2) It seems, according to Genesis 37, that at a certain point, the sons of Ishmael and the sons of Midian became one people (likely due to intermarriage). Therefore, the maternal lineage of Moses' two children stems from both Ishmael and Midian. As Moses himself was from the tribe of Levi (through Jacob and Isaac), we see in Moses' children the three-strand bloodline of Abraham represented.

The Exodus Generation of Egyptians

At the time of the Exodus, after seeing the destruction of Egypt's economy (due to the plagues) followed by the death of the nation's first-born sons, many Egyptians feared the God of Israel. God's intended purpose for demonstrating His awesomeness was to bring Egypt to repentance and recognition of the one true living God. Many Egyptians left Egypt with the people of Israel and joined God's family through circumcision and intermarriage, receiving inheritance in the promised land.

Rahab and Ruth

In the days of Joshua, Rahab, a gentile prostitute from Jericho, was not only spared from death, but she and her family were then numbered among God's people. Rahab was the mother of Boaz. Boaz married Ruth, another gentile woman from Moab. Ruth's son was Obed, the father of Jesse, the father of King David. (Matthew 1:5,6) These two women from foreign gentile nations were sovereignly chosen by God in response to their great faith and love and included in the redemptive story and bloodline of Jesus Christ himself "the Root and Offspring of David." (Revelation 22:6)

The Birth and Ministry of Jesus Christ

When Christ was born, the nations came to worship him. Persian Magi (a cast of priest in Zoroastrianism) presented precious gifts to him. Even at His birth, Christ was inviting the nations. As a little boy, Jesus was sent to Egypt not only to find refuge; I believe it was in His heart to visit Egypt with His hidden glory, inviting the rest of the Egyptian family to the promise of the Father.

In Jesus's final commissioning to the disciples, He clearly instructed them to go into all the earth, baptising and discipling nations into his name. (Matthew 28:18-20)

Before going out, they were instructed to wait for the Holy Spirit, the promise of the Father. On the Day of this visitation, Pentecost, it must have been shocking for the disciples (and everyone else around them) to hear one another speak in the languages of Gentile nations. It is remarkable to note that the first three languages listed in Acts 2 are languages from people groups in the region of Iran: Parthians, Medes and Elamites. I like to think that Jesus was responding to the Magi's visit by honouring them with the gift of His Holy Spirit. In that moment, God was actively seeking not only the Persians, but all the nations, inviting them to His family.

Through the reconciling work of the cross and the work of His Spirit—referenced by Paul as the Spirit of adoption —all the nations can now cry out together, "Abba, Father." Ethnicity is not what matters before God. What matters is that all who have been baptised by the same Spirit of God, which is what makes us sons and daughters of the Father and co-heirs with the Son, have become members of the same Family.(Romans 8:14-17)

In this new covenant, it's no longer about being in the direct bloodline of Abraham, or the external evidence of faith through circumcision; but rather about being grafted into the family of God through the blood of Jesus. It's the circumcision of the heart unto repentance that enables us by His grace to become eternal members of His family. (Ephesians 2:11-14)

ISRAEL, BORN IN EGYPT, RAISED IN IRAN

Until the time that his word came to pass, the word of the Lord tested him. (Psalm 105:19)

Section 2
God's People

"When Israel was a child, I loved him and out of Egypt I called My son."

(Hosea 11:1)

In a very poetic and beautiful depiction, Psalm 105 sums up hundreds of years of history of the people of God as they go in and out of Egypt. This psalm will serve as our guideline for this section as we stop at the different stations highlighted here to gain understanding of the significance of the role of Egypt in the journey of God's people.

"He is the Lord our God; His judgments are in all the earth. He remembers His covenant forever, the word which He commanded for a thousand generations, the covenant which He made with Abraham and His oath to Isaac and confirmed it to Jacob for a statute, to Israel as an everlasting covenant, saying, 'To you I will give the land of Canaan as the allotment of your inheritance,' when they were few in number, indeed very few and strangers in it. When they went from one nation to another, from one kingdom to another people, He permitted no one to do them wrong; yes, He rebuked kings for their sakes, saying, 'Do not touch My anointed ones and do My prophets no harm.' Moreover, He called for a famine in the land; He destroyed all the provision of bread. He sent a man before them—Joseph—who was sold as a slave. They hurt his feet with fetters, he was laid in irons. Until the time that his word came to pass, the word of the Lord tested him. The king sent and released him, the ruler of the people let him go free. He made him lord of his house and ruler of all his possessions, to bind his princes at his pleasure and teach his elders wisdom. Israel also came into Egypt and Jacob dwelt in the land of Ham. He increased His people greatly, and made them stronger than their enemies... He sent Moses His servant and Aaron whom He had chosen. They performed His signs among them and wonders in the land of Ham... He also destroyed all the firstborn in their land, the first of all their strength. He also brought them out with silver and gold and there was none feeble among His tribes... He brought out His people with joy, His chosen ones with gladness. He gave them the lands of the Gentiles and they inherited the labour of the nations, that they might observe His statutes and keep His laws. Praise the Lord!" (Psalm 105)

ISRAEL, BORN IN EGYPT, RAISED IN IRAN

In Egypt, genuine faith is tested and proven, resulting in the birthing of callings, destinies and nations.

Chapter 4

Egypt: Where Faith Is Tested

God's Patriarch

*"Get out of your country, from your family and from your
father's house to a land that I will show you. I will make
you a great nation and I will bless you and make your
name great and you shall be a blessing. I will bless those
who bless you and I will curse him who curses you and in
you all the families of the earth will be blessed."*
(Genesis 12:1-3)

This is the first recorded conversation between God and
Abraham, who was still called Abram at the time. God
gives him a promise. The essence of this promise is that
Abram's life will be a blessing to all nations and peoples.
God calls Abram out of a land, out of a family and out of a
household. Had he remained in the place where God
found him, he would not have been able to walk out the
fullness of his destiny. He had to move out before he
could enter into the promise; he had to step out of the
comfortable and familiar and step into the challenges of
the unknown.

God wanted to reveal His heart as the Father of the
Nations. To accomplish this, He chose one man, changed
his name[18] and through his life-journey God displayed His
deep desire for the families of the earth to come into the
Father's House, a House for all nations. (Isaiah 56:7)
God's plan wasn't limited to Abraham's original bloodline
or immediate family, but rather extended to "bless all the
families of the earth". This one man, chosen by God

because of his faith and obedience, became the foundation upon which the whole Judeo-Christian faith is built. Seeking God's will, Abram and his barren wife, Sarah, obeyed and started their journey, travelling all the way from Iraq to Canaan and down to Egypt.

Egypt, the Land of Testing

"There was a famine in the Land and Abram went to Egypt to dwell there." (Genesis 12:10)

The first time Egypt is mentioned in the Bible is after Abram responds to his encounter with God, which set the trajectory for his life for the next one hundred years. God had just promised him a multitude of descendants and a land filled with milk and honey. But reality hits hard! Abram is now confronted with the exact opposite: childless in a barren, fruitless land. To deal with this crisis, God sends him to Egypt.

For some reason, Abram lies about Sarah, saying that she is his sister and not his wife. Is it possible that considering his impossible situation, his shame, fear and unbelief manifest as soon as he arrives to Egypt? Was he trying to hide the shame of being childless at his age?

Shame and fear are two of the most powerful weapons the enemy uses against us to hinder us from walking in the fullness of God's purposes in our lives. They cause us to be drawn inward, focusing on what we cannot do, rather than outward on what God can do. Unfortunately, many people fall into this trap and miss out on God's best.

What did God want by sending Abram to Egypt? Was He intentionally allowing him to face his unbelief to make him an overcomer? Was He moulding him as the father of faith before He would become the father of nations? In Egypt, genuine faith is tested and proven, resulting in the birthing of callings, destinies and nations. Abraham, Joseph, Moses and even Jesus endured extended seasons of testing in Egypt before they each walked out the fullness of their calling.

The Covenant Promise

We do not know how long Abram lived in Egypt but even years later, in his second encounter with the Lord, we can sense the lingering wrestle in his heart: "What will you give me, seeing I go childless and the heir of my house is Eleazar of Damascus?" You can sense the deep pain engraved in this question: "Look, you have given me no offspring [as if God did not notice that]; indeed, one who is born [a servant] in my house is my heir." God kindly responds, countering all his doubts: "This one will not be your heir, but one that comes out of your body." In that moment, Abram was finally transformed: "And he believed in the Lord and He accounted it to him for righteousness." (Genesis 15:2-6)

Abram's righteousness was attributed to him because he believed the promise regarding future descendants; but he could still not quite fathom how and when the land would come. He asks, "How shall I know I will inherit it?" In response, God enters into a covenant with him, guaranteeing the fulfilment of His word.[19]

God's answer to Abram's question was not exactly what he was expecting to hear. "Abram, before you and your descendants inherit the land which will border the river of Egypt to the river of the Euphrates, they will actually be slaves for four hundred years." God conceals the details, cryptically saying only that his descendants would be "strangers in a land that is not their own". Those who have read ahead already know that this happens in Egypt.

In the covenantal act of cutting the pieces of the different animals, God was showing Abram that it will take a covenant of blood to bring this promise to fulfilment. It will ultimately be God's own Son, hanging on a wooden cross, with his blood pouring down, that will guarantee the fulfilment of the promise to Abraham and all his natural and spiritual children.

Now, even in the wake of a powerful encounter marking the promise of God, Abram (and Sarai) endeavour to make their own contribution to the promise. Trying to circumnavigate her barrenness, Sarai gives Abram her handmaiden, Hagar (an Egyptian who joined Abram's household when in Egypt), to bear a child. Abram and Sarai become the new parents of an Egyptian boy, Ishmael. (Genesis 16:1-4)

Egypt is now in Abram's bloodline; the first among the "families of the earth" to be included in Abram's blessing. Is this why God sent Abram to Egypt in the first place?

The Sign of the Covenant

Thirteen years after the birth of Ishmael, God appears to Abram another time to confirm (yet again) the covenant regarding the descendants and the land. God now establishes the covenant with an immediate, significant and lasting sign in Abram's spirit, soul, and body. His name is changed and he is left with a permanent mark in his flesh.

1 - A Name Change

God changes Abram's name to Abraham[20]. The intention was not to make the name sound better by adding another syllable, but rather indicate that Abraham now had a new "calling". God was declaring (paraphrasing): "Your new identity, based on my promise, is that you are a father; a father of many. You are going to have many natural and multitudes of spiritual children. From this moment on, you take on a new identity as a father of many nations. This is how people will recognise you from today. Not only that, I am also changing your wife's name from Sarai to Sarah because she shall be a mother of nations; kings of peoples shall be from her." (Genesis 17:4-6, 15-16)

2 - The Mark in the Flesh by Circumcision

God brings another sign into the equation; something much more personal (and painful) than a name change. Abraham is commanded to be circumcised, along with every male in his household, and to observe this custom in all future generations (Genesis 17:10). Through circumcision, these men and their posterity would all be partakers of the blessings of this covenant and would bring to remembrance the faithfulness of God, who keeps His promises.

This sign, because it was not limited to a biological transfer, was an expression of God's desire to forge a family from the nations. Any people could become partakers of the blessings of this covenant if they would carry this mark as a sign in their flesh and in the flesh of the following generations. (Genesis 17:13,14; Exodus 12:48)

Ishmael, Abraham's only son at the time, was circumcised the very same day with Abraham. God could have chosen to exclude Ishmael from this blessing. He could have simply waited to give the covenant of circumcision until after Isaac was born (only one year later) or after Ishmael left the household. But, no, it was God's intention to include Ishmael and make him and his descendants partakers of the blessing and covenant of Abraham. The sign in his flesh was a sign of belonging; Ishmael belonged to the family of God. (Genesis 17:23-27)

As the story develops, there is no question that Isaac was chosen by God to carry the covenant (carrying within it the seed of the Messiah). Some would then argue that because Ishmael was the first born, he should have been the carrier of the covenant. Others would argue that Ishmael was an illegitimate son and this is why he was not the carrier of the covenant. However, we see that God, nonetheless, blessed Ishmael and marked him as belonging to the family.

God also affirms to Abraham that He will establish His covenant with Sarah's son. God is committed to His word and His divine order. In this sense, God's choice for Isaac was, perhaps, not so much about Isaac as it was about Sarah. Sarah, not Hagar, was the one chosen to carry the son of promise. Therefore, it is through Sarah's descendants that the seed goes forth. (Genesis 17:15-19)

It is remarkable to consider that Emmanuel's first appearance to someone in human history was to an Egyptian slave.

Chapter 5

Egypt: Where Sons Are Called
God's Maiden

The story of Ishmael and Isaac is also the story of their two mothers, one from Iraq and one from Egypt. Their journeys intersect at their relationship to Abraham. As we follow their story over generations, we see God's wisdom in bringing them together and the blessing they both carried in their wombs.

Who is Hagar?

The Bible doesn't say much about Hagar's life before she joined Abraham's household. We know that she is Egyptian and was most likely sold as a slave to Abraham when he lived in Egypt. We learn about her for the first time from Sarah's lips.

"Now Sarai, Abram's wife, had borne him no children. And she had an Egyptian maidservant whose name was Hagar. So, Sarai said to Abram, 'The Lord has restrained me from bearing children. Please, go into my maid; perhaps I shall obtain children by her.' And Abram heeded the voice of Sarai. Then Sarai, Abram's wife, took Hagar her maid, the Egyptian and gave her to her husband Abram to be his wife ... So he went into Hagar, and she conceived..." (Genesis 16:1-4)

When Hagar became pregnant, pride crept into her heart and she despised Sarah's barrenness. In turn, Sarah

71

became jealous and angry. Sarah's mistreatment of Hagar pushed her to flee to the desert. We can see that the strife and jealousy that later existed between the descendants of Isaac and Ishmael started way before these boys were born, it started in the hearts of their mothers.

In Hebrew, Hagar's name means "flight" or "forsaken"; similarly in Arabic, it means "immigrated". Her name was more than fitting; it foreshadowed her destiny. Hagar immigrated from Egypt, her homeland, becoming a slave in Canaan. Later, she fled into the wilderness, escaping Sarah's harshness. Eventually, she was forsaken by Abraham, thus fulfilling all three meanings of her name. Though she had a difficult life, God had seen her and known her before it all happened and He was planning something glorious for her and her offspring.

We do not know how long Hagar was in the desert, pregnant with her master's child, but we know that she was not alone. There she has, what is, in my opinion, one of the most beautiful encounters in the whole Bible when "the Angel of the Lord found her." (Genesis 16:7)

Who is the Angel of the Lord?

Most scholars agree that this "visitation" is a description of Hagar encountering the pre-incarnate Christ. This occurrence in Scripture is called theophany or Christophany, describing an appearance of God in flesh before the historical incarnation and birth of Christ. Some examples include an appearance to Abraham to address the concern of Sodom; to Moses in the burning bush commissioning him to go back to Egypt; to Samson's parents, announcing the unique child they were to raise; and in the flames with Daniel's friends, honouring their courage and loyalty of heart. (Genesis 18, Exodus 3, Judges 13, Daniel 3)

This occurrence is significant in that it is the first time scripture uses the term "the angel of the Lord". It is remarkable to consider that Emmanuel's first appearance to someone in human history was to an Egyptian slave. Christ, who would be born generations later through Sarah's bloodline, was now appearing to the mother of Ishmael, preserving her and the child in her womb: Abraham's first son.

God could have easily corrected Abraham's "mistake" by simply not intervening in this situation, allowing Hagar and her baby to die in the desert. But no, the Angel of the Lord sought her out and found her, in her desperate condition, hopeless and without a plan. In the desert, Christ reveals Himself to Hagar as "the God who sees" and as "the God who hears" and He promises her a hopeful future, blessing her son and his future generations. (Genesis 16:9-12)

But why were Hagar and Ishmael so important to the Lord? Why was it necessary that He himself (not just an angel or other messenger) come down to intervene? We will look at further details of the unfolding answer but, for now, it is enough to say that Ishmael's survival was critical to the overall plan of God, even in setting the stage for the Incarnation of Christ Himself.

The God Who Sees: A new name

As is always the case, when heaven touches earth, this one meeting between God and Hagar transformed her heart and destiny forever. Surely, she had heard much about the God of Abraham, but this moment of personal encounter opened her eyes and positioned her life to experience the impossible. I am sure she was in total awe and fascination with this God. A veil was lifted and she was able to see, for the first time, the One who sees. I can hear her soul echoing the words of Job: "I have heard of You by the hearing of the ear, but now my eyes see You." (Job 42:5)

Not only did this encounter change Hagar, but it also changed the way she viewed and experienced God. The essence of God does not change (He is the "I am") but in this moment, Hagar had a revelation of who God is and she named Him accordingly: the God who sees. Hagar becomes the first person in biblical history to give God a new name. "You see me in my affliction and my distress; you know me. You know how to find me, how to reach and rescue me, how to give me hope and a future: you are 'Lahai Roi.'" (Genesis 16:13,14)

I love this exchange between God and Hagar. I can imagine a smile on the face of the Angel of the Lord as He discloses the name of her son. "You shall call his name Ishmael.[21] Every time you call your son's name, you will remember me and this moment, recalling that your God is not only a God who sees you in your afflictions, but also a God who is attentive to your voice."

Because of this encounter and the hope of the promise given, courage rose and she made the choice to return and submit to Sarah's harshness. Abraham must have been delighted to see her and to hear how God had miraculously intervened and named his son in Hagar's womb.

The Promise to Sarah

The biblical record picks up the story years later when Abraham is ninety-nine years old and Ishmael is thirteen. At this time, God gives Abraham the covenant of circumcision (as was discussed earlier) and confirms His promises, that Sarah will still conceive at the age of ninety. "As for Sarai your wife, you shall not call her name Sarai, but Sarah... And I will bless her and also give you a son by her; and she shall be a mother of nations; kings of peoples shall be from her." (Genesis 17:15-16)

Abraham's immediate response to this renewed promise was laughter and unbelief. "Lord, this is the funniest thing I've ever heard, ha, ha, ha... that's a really good joke! I have my son now; you gave him to me as you promised. Let Ishmael live before you... forget about this other impossible situation. I am content as things are." God's response was a quick and sharp: NO! "Sarah your wife will bear you a son and you shall call him Isaac; I will establish my everlasting covenant with him and for his descendants after him. I will visit you again next year and Sarah will have a son." (paraphrased from Genesis 17:19,21)

Family shake up

God's promise to Abraham came to pass. Sarah did conceive and gave birth to a miracle son. It wasn't a joke after all. The birth of Isaac, however, caused a massive shift in the family dynamics. For fourteen years, Sarah and Abraham considered Ishmael to be their own son. But now that Isaac was around, "the bondwoman's son" not only did not matter to Sarah anymore, but she was irritated by him, she wanted him out of her house.

"Abraham made a great feast on the same day that Isaac was weaned. And Sarah saw that the son of Hagar the Egyptian, scoffing. Therefore, she said to Abraham, 'Cast out this bondwoman and her son; for the son of this bondwoman shall not be heir with my son...' God said to Abraham, 'Do not let it be displeasing in your sight... for in Isaac your seed shall be called. Yet I will also make a nation of the son of the bondwoman, because he is your seed.' So Abraham rose early in the morning and took bread and a skin of water; and putting it on her shoulder, he gave it and the boy to Hagar and sent her away. Then she departed and wandered in the Wilderness of Beersheba." (Genesis 21:8-14)

Ishmael's wound

Imagine you are fourteen years old, dearly beloved by your father. One morning you wake up, and your father, whom you adore, gives you a piece of bread and some water and sends you away from your home, away from his presence, forever. Overnight, you are left alone, homeless and fatherless; left to wander in the desert; left to hunger and thirst; left to die. That was Ishmael's experience after the birth of Isaac.

What was the level of pain triggered in Ishmael's heart that day? What were the kinds of questions that went through his mind? How intense were the emotions of confusion, betrayal and abandonment? Abraham's decision must have broken his heart. It must have created a very deep "father wound": a wound of separation from the father, a wound of desperation for a father he no longer had and a wound of longing to return home, to be with the family again.

Perhaps the only thing that made sense to him at that moment was that the source of all his pain was this new little baby. It was his fault. Hatred and revenge must have been bearing down on his heart. Perhaps he may have even had thoughts like, "One day, I will come back, get rid of this new baby and take back my inheritance."

Middle Eastern wound

Doesn't this sound like the sentiment within the Middle East today? Doesn't this resonate with the cries rising from the Israeli/Palestinian conflict? Perhaps, what is happening there today is, in some part, a manifestation of that ancient wound that was opened in Ishmael's heart thousands of years ago; a wound that is, unfortunately, still bleeding in the hearts of millions.

I believe that this "father-wound" manifests itself later within a pillar in Islam, denying the Fatherhood of God and the Sonship of Jesus Christ. One of the most foundational verses in the Qur'an, called by many as the "essence of the Quran", states, "God is one, He is absolute; He has not given birth and was not born, nor does He have an equal."[22] This is not only a theological statement of monotheism, but emphasises that God is not, nor can He be approached as, a father—the exact opposite of the essence of the gospel!

Hagar's cry

Déjà vu: alone in the desert, in the wilderness of Beersheba, Hagar and Ishmael were again in a dire and helpless situation. With no water left, no food, only faint shelter in the form of some shade from a nearby bush, Hagar distances herself from her son crying out: "I cannot watch the boy die..." Those tears were not only tears of pain and desperation, but I believe they were her cry of intercession for Ishmael to live. Hagar, who had already survived much affliction, lifted up her voice, wondering, if "the God who sees" would see her again; if "the God who hears" would hear her cry one more time. God did hear the boy crying and the Angel of the Lord called Hagar from heaven, saying, "What is the matter, Hagar? Do not be afraid; lift the boy up and take him by the hand, for I will make him into a great nation. Then God opened her eyes and she saw a well of water. So, she went and filled the skin with water and gave the boy a drink." (Genesis 21:17-19)

Water from the well

Following this account of Ishmael, the Bible intentionally makes a connecting point to the story of a particular well: the well of Beersheba. There was a conflict regarding the ownership of this well and when it was settled, Abraham made a treaty with Abimelech, whose name means "my father is king". Abraham said, "You will take these seven ewe lambs from my hand, that they may be my witness that I have dug this well. Therefore, he called that place Beersheba ... then Abraham planted a tamarisk tree in Beersheba and there, [he] called on the name of the Lord, the Everlasting God." (Genesis 21:30-33)

The biblical text is clear. Hagar was wandering in the wilderness of Beersheba. (Genesis 21:14). Of all the places that she could have run to, it is not improbable that Hagar ran to the same well that Abraham had dug. Although Abraham sent them away, God, in His providence, led Hagar and Ishmael to Abraham's water source. The boy's life was preserved and one could say that their heavenly father "who is King" provided a well for Hagar and Ishmael. Scripture says that God not only saved his life as He had promised Abraham but was with the boy as he grew up. His mother arranged for a wife for him from Egypt and God blessed Ishmael with twelve sons.[23] (Genesis 21:20-21; 25:12-16) Thus, Hagar became the grandmother of these twelve princes, who formed a great nation as God promised.

At the time of Abraham's death, the Bible says that Isaac and Ishmael buried their father together (Genesis 25:9), which implies they lived not only in proximity to each other, but their relationship was intact. I believe this picture has a prophetic significance for the future relationship between the sons of Isaac and sons of Ishmael. The prophet Isaiah affirms this as he mentions Ishmael's firstborn son Nebaioth and his brother Kedar among the nations that will be drawn into the glorious light of the Kingdom of God. (Isaiah 60:7ff)

Immediately after Abraham's death, Isaac relocates and goes to dwell by Beer Lahai Roi—the well of Hagar's first encounter. (Genesis 25:9,11) Of all the places he would want to live, he chose to live in the place where God encountered and comforted Hagar and his brother Ishmael. I picture the brothers walking shoulder to shoulder, grieving their beloved father, until they reach the spot where Ishmael points out the exact location where the Angel of the Lord saved his life. Desperate for comfort himself, Isaac sets up camp to carry on his father's legacy, drawing strength from this place of encounter, breakthrough and transformation.

Living Water for the sons of Ishmael

As we began this chapter talking about two mothers, I cannot help but think of two other mothers, introduced in the New Testament, whose stories and destinies were also deeply intertwined: Mary and Elizabeth. Instead of jealousy and strife, as in the case of Sarah and Hagar, we see a redemptive picture of great joy and mutual encouragement shared in their difficult circumstances. The fruit of these mothers' hearts toward each other is further evidenced in the relationship that Jesus and John had. John lived to see Jesus exalted; his joy was to see Jesus walk in the fullness of His destiny, giving his life in preparing the way for Him. Jesus loved and honoured John, humbly submitting to his ministry of baptism and honouring him among the people.

Jesus's life and ministry was destined to be the source of healing, not only for His immediate family (the family of Abraham), but for all nations, reconciling us back to the Father and into the family of Abraham. In Heaven's declaration over Jesus at His Baptism, we hear the truth of the Father-heart of God that confronts the orphan spirit in us all: "This is my Beloved Son in whom I am well pleased! (Matthew 3:17)

Though this message is foreign and even offensive to many people, especially to the sons of Ishmael around the world, it is the message that they need to hear; it is the Father they need to encounter; it is the sacrifice of the Son of God, Jesus, that they need to receive so that they also may have the right to become the beloved sons and daughters of God. (John 1:12)

Today in the Muslim world, people are coming to Christ in great numbers. One common experience that many have shared is encountering Jesus in a dream, a vision or some other supernatural way. It is remarkable to note that Jesus continues to interact with the descendants of Ishmael today in the same way he interacted with Hagar and Ishmael back then. He shows up, personally, letting them know that He sees and hears them; He heals their hearts and gives them Living Water. The Gospel is the only answer that can heal the wound of separation from the Father. It is the work of the Holy Spirit, through the blood of Jesus, that brings us back to the family. Whether Jew, Gentile, Muslim or otherwise, we can all belong to the family of God.

81

For you did not receive the spirit of bondage again to fear, but you received the Spirit of adoption by whom we cry out, "Abba Father". The Spirit Himself bears witness with our spirit that we are children of God, and if children, then heirs—heirs of God and joint heirs with Christ. (Romans 8:15-17)

I believe that this ancient story has relevance for us today. Hagar, as a mother, is a picture of an intercessor. Because she encountered the Lord face to face and was transformed, she refused to just concede to her circumstances, to let the child die in the wilderness. Rather, she poured out her last strength, crying out to the Lord, interceding for her son's life. In our generation, God is raising up spiritual "Hagars" to intercede for the sons of Ishmael to encounter the Living Water, to find healing and live, to be reconciled to the family and to come back to the Father's house.

Would you position your heart today to carry the descendants of Ishmael and Isaac, bringing them to the Well of Life? God is seeking voices to cry out for his estranged and wounded sons and daughters. Will you be one?[24]

ISRAEL, BORN IN EGYPT, RAISED IN IRAN

Joseph's destiny wasn't primarily determined by his brothers' jealousy. It was determined by God's sovereign leadership.

Chapter 6

Egypt: Where Destiny Is Realised
God's Dreamer

"Are we there yet? When will we get there? Why does it have to take so long? Why didn't we take the shortcut? Can we stop now?"

If you are a parent, like me, these are some of the questions that you and I get asked by our children when we are on a long car ride. After I get asked several of these by each of my six children, I find myself wondering why we even set out to go anywhere in the first place. Perhaps it would have just been simpler to stay in the predictable comfort of our home.

This is not just the case with kids. Adults also ask these questions all the time; maybe not on a car ride, but on the journey of life. We don't normally process delays well; we typically don't like it when others are in the driver's seat, taking us to an unknown location, or to a place we may already be convinced we do not like. We want to be in control, to decide on the destination and how fast we get there.

Joseph's journey to Egypt was not in a car, but on a camel's back through the scorching desert sun for several long weeks. His destination in Egypt was not a holiday weekend at the Red Sea, neither was it going to be the end of his affliction. It was only the beginning of years of detours and testing. He had a promise, that one day his brothers, who had just betrayed him, would kneel at his feet, honouring him. All of this seemed to be a distant dream as he faced an unpredictable future. Joseph's destiny, however, wasn't primarily determined by his brothers' jealousy. It was determined by God's sovereign leadership. God's plan had implications, not only for Joseph but also for his entire family as well as the surrounding nations for generations to come.

As we follow Joseph's journey, there are several important details we should pay attention to that shed significant light on God's heart and His plan for world redemption by involving all the sons of Abraham.

"So it came to pass, when Joseph had come to his brothers, that they stripped Joseph of his tunic of many colours. Then they took him and cast him into a pit ... they lifted their eyes and looked, and there was a company of Ishmaelites ... bearing spices, balm, and myrrh, on their way to carry them down to Egypt. So, Judah said to his brothers, 'What profit is there if we kill our brother and conceal his blood? Come and let us sell him to the Ishmaelites, and let not our hand be upon him, for he is our brother and our flesh.' And his brothers listened. Then Midianite traders passed by; so, the brothers pulled Joseph up and lifted him out of the pit and sold him to the Ishmaelites for twenty shekels of silver. And they took Joseph to Egypt." (Genesis 37:23-28)

There are two main questions we should answer here: Who is it that saved Joseph from being murdered? And, who carried Joseph to Egypt?

It was Judah who persuaded his brothers to sell Joseph to the traders instead of killing him. Judah was led by God to make a way for his brother to escape, not knowing that Joseph's survival was essential to the survival of the whole family and his own lineage. In this act, he was preserving the lineage of kings and ultimately the King of Kings, the Messiah, the Lion of the Tribe of Judah. Secondly, according to the scripture, the Bible uses two names interchangeably to describe the same people group: the Ishmaelites and the Midianites. The Ishmaelites are the descendants of Ishmael, the son of Abraham and Hagar. The Midianites are the descendants of Midian, the son of Abraham and Keturah. It seems that these two groups became one people, living in the land of Midian, on the East side of the Red Sea, in what is now part of Saudi Arabia.[25]

As we know, Ishmael was Isaac's older brother and Jacob was Isaac's son. That makes Ishmael Jacob's uncle and Joseph's great uncle. So those Ishmaelite traders were Joseph's cousins! One can only imagine what they could have talked about on their way to Egypt. Did they discover their blood relationship? Did they perhaps talk about how Joseph—being abandoned by his brothers— reminded them of the story of their grandfather, Ishmael, who had also been abandoned by Abraham? One outcast "son of Abraham" was now helping another outcast "son of Abraham", both playing a part in accomplishing God's promise to their Patriarch.

Through God's sovereign leadership, He was now joining the destinies of the sons of Isaac and the sons of Ishmael, allowing both to participate in the greatest story of redemption ever told. In this, God was honouring His word to Abraham regarding Ishmael. He was also bringing Isaac and Ishmael together, to be united in the fulfilment of God's promise to Abraham: that through his descendants, all the nations would be blessed. God's promises to Joseph were also being carried here. Ishmael was positioned by God to help Joseph, to carry him into his inheritance in Egypt. Without Ishmael, Joseph's dreams would have perished with him.

Just like Ishmael carried Joseph into his destiny, I believe the sons of Ishmael will again, in our generation, be used by God to carry, and even provoke, Israel to a holy jealousy for their own fullness, bringing them into their destiny. Many who have come to Christ from a Muslim background have testified that they have been given a supernatural love and burden for the salvation of Israel. What a testimony this will be to the Jewish people, when their neighbours, who once hated them are transformed by the love of God and are even willing to lay down their lives for them.[26]

Joseph's Second Robe

In the beginning of his life in Egypt, Joseph was sold as a slave to an Egyptian officer named Potiphar. It wasn't very long before he gained this man's favour and trust, being promoted as the steward of his whole household. God's Kingdom started to manifest through Joseph's life, even causing Potiphar's house to be blessed. His wife, however, was also mesmerised by Joseph and now he was facing persistent and almost oppressive pressure as she enticed him day after day to commit adultery. Though the Law had not yet been given, God's standard for purity was written on Joseph's heart by the Spirit, and he persistently refused to give in to this temptation.

Finally, the lady forced herself upon him and in doing so, she pulled off his robe as he ran to escape her gropings. To revenge her humiliation, she stirred lies and accusations against him—a common strategy the enemy uses—which resulted in Joseph's imprisonment.

This was the second time he lost a robe. What he didn't know at the time, was that God was preparing him to receive a third robe of ultimate favour and authority. God's promise to Joseph was going to continue to test him, though, actively refining him and making him stronger, before it would become reality in his life.

"...Until His word came to pass the word of the Lord tested [Joseph]." (Psalm 105:19)

"Joseph is a fruitful bough, a fruitful bough by a well, his branches run over the wall. The archers have bitterly grieved him and shot him and hated him, but his bow remains in strength and the arms of his hands were made strong by the hands of the Mighty God of Jacob, from there is the shepherd the stone of Israel." (Genesis 49:22)

Isn't this similar in our own walk with the Lord? When He gives us a promise, there is usually a delay before it is fulfilled and sometimes the fulfilment is realised in stages. Why does God do that? In the delay, our hearts are tested, our motives are purified, our character is matured; in the process, we are equipped to then rightfully steward the gift when He gives it. We must not be naive though. When it comes to pursuing the calling and the destiny of the Lord, resistance, temptation, lies and accusations are to be expected; we must remain strong as Joseph did.

Joseph's third robe

In prison, God again granted favour. The keeper of the prison appointed Joseph as steward of the prison. Even the inmates trusted him with their dreams. One night, Pharoah's butler and baker each had a dream. Joseph offered an interpretation, which came to pass only three days later, on Pharoah's birthday. (Genesis 40)

I can't help but to consider Joseph's feelings, wondering about his own dreams. These men's dreams came to pass after only three days; why was he still waiting, after so many years? Was there some pain and confusion in Joseph's heart as he petitioned the butler to remember him when he went before Pharaoh? Unfortunately, two more years would pass before he remembered to commend Joseph to Pharaoh. But Joseph's destiny was not hinging on the butler's memory; rather, on God's perfect timing.

Finally, the breakthrough—in the form of two dreams given to Pharaoh in one night. I want to highlight the remarkable orchestration of this theme of dreams. In this storyline, the Bible records six dreams: two that Joseph has about himself, two that he interprets for the butler and the baker, and two that he interprets for Pharaoh. Each two sets of dreams were clearly given by God and though they were experienced over a span of decades, they were all going to collide in one single day, the latter bringing about the fulfilment of the former! God would bring Joseph's dreams to pass as He used Joseph to bring understanding to Pharaohs own dreams. (Genesis 41)

As Pharaoh searches for someone to interpret his dreams, God stirs the butler's memory to mention to Pharaoh Joseph's abilities. Joseph is brought in to be tested and he confidently declares: "God will give Pharaoh an answer of peace." As Joseph waits upon the Lord for the interpretation, God gives him a download of wisdom and understanding. The dreams meaning: God will bring seven years of surplus to be followed by seven years of famine in Egypt; it was critical that the nation be prepared not only for the time of famine, but to become the breadbasket for the whole region.

As Pharaoh hears the interpretation and the proposed action plan, he marvels, saying, "Who can we find that has the spirit of God more than this man?" He gives Joseph his royal ring, a royal robe and appoints him to be the second in command of the whole nation.

What must have Joseph felt in that moment? Years and years of waiting, suffering, betrayal, slavery, imprisonment and loss of reputation were all coming to an end. Not only was his anguish ending, but his dreams were being fulfilled—all in one day.

I imagine him having a flashback to the years of his beautiful childhood, enjoying his father's affections, recalling the treasured multicolour robe. I can imagine him feeling the pain of separation, not knowing if he will ever again see his father. I can imagine his heart again moving in surrender, as he recalls how he gained his second robe of favour as a slave in a foreign land but losing it to the hands of a disgruntled woman when he chose to submit to purity in the fear of the Lord.

I can imagine the weight of God's presence and glory resting upon him as Pharaoh placed that royal robe on him. In that moment, God was healing his heart and giving him a new beginning. This royal robe was an outward expression of the righteousness that he had walked in, in the secret place for many years. He had been tested, tried and found worthy of the dreams; the promises given so long ago.

In that moment, the wisdom of the ways of the kingdom of God was justified in his life. It was all worth it. The pain and the sacrifice was worth it. It was worth the wait for the word of the Lord to come to pass!

Overnight, Joseph became the prime minister of Egypt, one of the greatest ancient civilisations. Through his life, fully submitted to the will of God, Joseph became a channel for the Lord, and opened a gate in the spirit for God's ways to flow throughout the land. Though he was amid a pagan society, God opened a window for the nation of Egypt to be delivered from this system and come under the blessing of God's leadership.

God was positioning and inviting Egypt to provide for, nurture and preserve the ancestors of the Messiah and to release the nation of Israel into her destiny. Thus, the fulfilment of Joseph's dreams was connected to what God wanted to do through Pharaoh and Egypt. This was not merely a convergence of independent storylines; it was one storyline. God took the time to arrange circumstances and to position people so He could give the greatest breakthrough—a Kairos moment[27]—to everyone, in just the right time and place.

Like Joseph, who was a prototype, the Lord will bring kingdom answers amid natural disasters and international calamity through yielded vessels. As His friends, we are being prepared, sometimes over decades, through the mundane and the pressures "until His word comes to pass." He takes the time to teach us, to fill us with His Spirit, to cultivate wisdom and understanding so that in critical moments we can bring in the wisdom of God and His "answer of peace." (Genesis 41:16)

God is in the driver's seat! He knows the destination, the detours, the stops and the arrival time. He is leading history, commissioning forerunners to lead the way so that others can follow into God's purposes. Those forerunners have been tested and tried, they have suffered betrayal and loss, they have chosen the low way of humility in the secret place; they have learned to abide in Christ and be found in Him. They have persevered through prayer and fasting, continuing to believe the promises: "Looking unto Jesus, the author and the perfecter of our faith." (Hebrews 12:2)

God will prove Himself faithful as He positions them to confront the Pharaohs of their day. He will show Himself strong on their behalf and cause His glory to be revealed in the darkest hour of human history.

In Egypt, at Joseph's table, God was restoring the family order.

Chapter 7

Egypt: Where Generations Reconcile

God's Family

When it comes to important occasions in our lives, be it a graduation, marriage, the birth of a child, a promotion, or, in my case, finishing this book, the people that we desire to celebrate with usually include family and our closest friends. Our joy is never complete without these precious ones alongside. If a close family member was unable to participate in a very special occasion, due to death or some other circumstance, their absence is usually marked with a sense of remorse or sadness, even amid the most joyful moment of one's life.

When Joseph received his epic promotion, his father was absent. None of his family was there to celebrate with him, nor were they present to comfort him for all the years of pain he had endured alone. Even though his personal journey was vindicated as he received the highest honour of Egypt, in reality his joy was incomplete and his dream was not fully realised because its fullness was dependent on the rest of his family walking it out together with him.

What Joseph did not know at the time was that God had orchestrated the famine to guide his family down to Egypt, where they would be reunited. God still had a much bigger plan for Joseph and for this plan to be accomplished, his family had to be with him. In Egypt, they were reunited, reconciled, multiplied and released into their ultimate destiny together. God wasn't just planning one man's story of success. He was planning the birth of a whole nation.

When it comes to a sense of family, the people of Egypt have a special God-given "gift" within their culture and society. If you have ever visited Egypt, you immediately notice how warm the people are and how welcoming they are to bring you, as a stranger, into their homes. There's a saying in Egypt ("Egypt is the mother of the world") as Egypt has a natural tendency to adopt sons and daughters. The Egyptian way of saying, "Welcome" is "Ahlan wa Sahlan" (أهلا وسهلا), which basically means, "You have become family and you have room in our midst." Perhaps this was one reason God wanted to reunite Joseph's family in Egypt. He was bringing his family there to birth reconciliation and healing in this land of family, a womb of nations.

Dealing with the famine

For seven years, Joseph was administrating the crops and the wealth of Egypt. Through his leadership, under God's wisdom, Egypt became the breadbasket of the ancient world. There was abundance for seven years but then the harsh reality of the famine impacted everyone, far and near.

Even in Canaan, for Jacob and his family to survive they had to bring grain from Egypt. Jacob sent his sons, all except Benjamin, to explore this possibility. In Egypt, they unknowingly stood before their brother Joseph, now the overseer of Egypt's economy, requesting grain. Immediately, he recognised them. The last time he had seen them was from the bottom of the waterless pit, with anguish in his soul. Now he was standing as a ruler in Egypt with his brothers bowing before him, just as he had seen in his dreams so many years before. (Genesis 37:5-11)

In the moment, he chose to hide his identity as he was emotionally overwhelmed. He left the room to weep when he heard his brothers converse with remorse over the way they treated him: "For we saw the anguish of his soul when he pleaded with us and we would not hear." (Genesis 42:21)

As Joseph gathered himself, he decided to let them go, but kept their brother Simeon in custody until they returned with their brother Benjamin - as proof that they are honest men and not spies.

Brothers heal

We don't know how long the grain supply lasted, but eventually Jacob's sons had to go back to Egypt. Traumatised by the thought of losing yet another son, Jacob was not willing to let go of Benjamin: "You have bereaved me, Joseph is no more, Simeon is no more and you want to take Benjamin!" (Genesis 42:36)

But, after much negotiation, Judah (again) brokered a deal guaranteeing the return of Benjamin and Jacob reluctantly agreed. (Genesis 43:8-10)

As they returned to Egypt, the brothers fell before Joseph. As soon as Joseph saw his brother Benjamin, his heart was moved deeply and he had to dismiss himself again to weep. Then he washed his face, restrained himself and invited them for a meal at his house. The brothers were dumbfounded at this act of hospitality, as they sat down in position according to their age, oldest to youngest. In Egypt, at Joseph's table, God was restoring the family order.

After the meal, they were allowed to leave, only to be pursued again by Joseph's servants, who accused them of stealing Joseph's special cup. Benjamin had been framed (by Joseph) and the cup was found in his sack. The brothers tore their clothes in grief as they knew the implications of this: Benjamin's imprisonment would lead to their father's death. The worst-case scenario had happened!

In this critical moment, Judah lifted his voice to intercede on behalf of Benjamin, pleading with Joseph to take him as a prisoner instead of Benjamin: "Since Jacob's life is bound up on the lad's life, it will happen when he sees that he is not with us that he will die and we will bring the grey hair of your servant, our father, with sorrow to the grave." (Genesis 44:31)

Hearing Judah's intercession, Joseph lost all his restraint as the pent-up emotions burst from the depths of his being. In a flood of tears, he wept and wept as years of pain were finally being released and healed in his brothers' embrace. What was it about Judah's appeal that triggered the breakthrough? Joseph probably had a tender spot for Judah in his heart. After all, Judah was the one that saved his life, pleading with the others to not kill him but rather sell him to the Ishmaelites. (Genesis 37:27)

Joseph must have thought often about Judah and what he did, and what would have happened had he not intervened. In that moment, a deep pain was being healed, as Joseph revealed himself to his brothers: "I am Joseph your brother, do not be grieved, or angry. It was God who sent me here." (Genesis 45:4,5)

God's commitment to the generations

Meanwhile, Jacob was at home, alone, wondering if his sons would ever come back, wondering if he would see Benjamin again. After months of waiting, one day, in the distance, he sees an Egyptian caravan with horses and chariots. I can imagine that there was a lot of emotion as Jacob's sons saw their father in the distance, shouting over each other, "Joseph is Alive, He is Alive, He is alive!" I am sure Jacob could hardly contain his emotions, as he saw all his sons, including Benjamin, return in new clothes, bearing gifts. With hope rising as his spirit was revived with the news, the aged Jacob found strength within a determination to make the journey to Egypt to be reunited to his beloved Joseph. (Genesis 45:27,28)

Back to Beersheba

"So, Israel took his journey with all that he had and came to Beersheba... and God said, 'I am the God of your father...do not fear to go down to Egypt, for I will make of you a great nation there. I will go down with you to Egypt and I will also surely bring you up again...' then Jacob arose from Beersheba." (Genesis 46:1-5)

This stop that Jacob made at the well of Beersheba is very significant. This was the well that his grandfather, Abraham, had dug. It is likely that it was the same well that nurtured and saved Ishmael from death. Now, as Jacob is at a major crossroads in his life, God appears to him at the same well to show him the destiny of His people for generations to come. The well of Beersheba is a place of divine providence, protection and provision. It is the place where God once again assures His people regarding His commitment and plans for their family. We see him weaving a beautiful thread through this storyline, as He provided water that sustained generations. He saved Ishmael to save Joseph to save Jacob to birth the nation of Israel—it all connects around this well.

Father and son reunited

Unable to wait for their arrival, Joseph got on his chariot and raced out to meet his father. His heart pounding, his thoughts racing as he stopped the chariot, he could hardly breathe as he fell at his father's neck and the washing flood of tears continued. You can sense the overwhelming nature of this reunion, as Jacob utters, after a long embrace, that he can now die, having seen his son's face. (Genesis 46:30)

So, Jacob's family is reunited in Egypt, this mother-nation. A new chapter of the family history is written as Jacob stands before Pharaoh, releasing the blessing of the Patriarchal Covenant and establishing God's purposes over the land of Egypt for future generations. (Genesis 47:7)

The family legacy

Years passed and, on his deathbed, Jacob blessed his twelve sons. From Egypt, as the nation of Israel was in her infancy, Jacob prophesied, marking each tribe for what they were to become. You can find his beautiful words in Genesis 49, but I would like to highlight a few of these blessings.

Judah

"Judah, you are he whom your brothers shall praise; the sceptre shall not depart from Judah nor the lawgiver between his feet until shiloh comes and to him shall be the obedience of the people... He washed his garments in wine and his clothes in the blood of grapes, his eyes darker than wine and teeth whiter than milk." (Genesis 49: 8-12)

Judah plays a significant prophetic role in this journey. He causes Joseph's life to be spared instead of being murdered. He reasons with Jacob to let Benjamin go to Egypt, offering his own life as the guarantee. He intercedes on behalf of Benjamin, who was accused in Egypt, compelling Joseph to reveal his true identity. He was the one sent ahead of the family to meet Joseph and to scout out the land of Goshen.

In foreshadowing the characteristics of saviour, intercessor, mediator and a way-finder, he personally walked out a dimension of the destiny placed upon his lineage. Out of Judah would come forth the Saviour of the world, the Great Hight Priest, the only Way, the Truth and the Life; the Lion of the tribe of Judah, our Lord Jesus Christ.

In the blessing of Judah, we discover some of the oldest references to the Messiah in Scripture. The sceptre is a sign of the authority of the king who is to come, who will receive the obedience of the nations. His clothes are washed in blood, pointing to His atoning work on the cross. It would take many generations for this word to come to pass, but it is significant to note that out of Egypt, not only did God call His son, Israel, but He also declared the destiny of His only begotten Son, the promised Messiah. (Hosea 11:1)

Thus, through his boldness and courage, Judah was a forerunner used by God to preserve the lineage of all Israel. His intercession before Jacob and Joseph, on behalf of Benjamin, bound them together. It was the tribe of Judah and Benjamin that would later become the southern kingdom. With the Levites, they were the only remaining tribes that returned to Israel after the exile, making way for the coming of the Messiah.

Manasseh and Ephraim: The Egyptian tribes

"And now your two sons, Ephraim and Manasseh, who were born to you in the land of Egypt ... are mine; as Reuben and Simeon ... let my name be named upon them, And the name of my fathers Abraham and Isaac; And let them grow into a multitude in the midst of the earth." (Genesis 48:5,15,16)

Manasseh and Ephraim, the sons of Joseph and his Egyptian wife, were wealthy and privileged. They were the elite of the elite. They had grown up as Egyptian princes and probably played with Pharaoh's sons. Now, they were being adopted by Jacob as his own.

As a result of this blessing, the tribes of Manasseh and Ephraim, who were ethnically and culturally Egyptian, became an integral part of God's people. Only a few generations later, their children lost their royal privilege, becoming slaves, leaving with Moses in the Exodus and inheriting land at the time of Joshua. These two tribes, with Egyptian ancestry, possessed one-sixth of the allotted inheritance in the promised land—more tangible evidence that God desires a family from the nations!

Jacob's funeral

When Jacob died, according to royal Egyptian traditions, he was mummified, a process that took forty days. The whole nation of Egypt mourned him for seventy days (Genesis 50:2-3)[28]. As he had promised, Joseph went to bury Jacob in Canaan. Not only did Joseph's family travel, but so did Pharaoh's servants, the elders of his house and the elders of the land of Egypt. They went up with chariots and horsemen to honour Israel. It was a very great gathering. In fact, the people of the land saw many Egyptians mourning, so they thought this was an Egyptian funeral procession and called it "abel Mizraim." (Genesis 50:7-11)

In their journey from Egypt to Canaan, they went all the way beyond the Jordan together. In other words, the

Egyptians and the children of Israel went together in honour of Jacob to the land of their promised inheritance. It was a prophetic picture of how Egypt was destined to partner with God to bring fulfilment to the promise. But we know how the story goes.

It is unbelievable to see the contrast between this scenario in Genesis 50 and that in Exodus 14. Here, the nation mourns and Israel is escorted by the Egyptian military (a sign of honour) to bury their patriarch. Only a few generations later, due to deception and pride, Egypt's face turned away from blessing God's people, chasing them down a similar path, using the same military might and seeking to enslave them again. The first time Israel carried Jacob's bones in honour, the second time they carried Joseph's bones in flight!

Getting perspective

Joseph had acquired a divine perspective. Rather than allowing bitterness and hatred to fill the void in his soul, he chose to forgive and embrace the painful journey he had walked as the vehicle through which God was accomplishing His purposes. He understood that his brothers, though their hearts and actions were wrong and sinful, were still in the hands of God. He realised that through Judah, his life had been spared to then turn and spare their lives and the destiny of the family of Abraham, Isaac and Jacob. (Genesis 50:20,21)

You see, it's not always just about you. Your personal dream and destiny are connected to a family story and a Kingdom story. Our personal family units are connected to the larger family of God across the nations. One family story is intricately tied to the other stories. Thus, we all have a responsibility to walk in humility, repentance, forgiveness and reconciliation, so we can all reach the fullness. And just like Jacob, our Father's heart would be fully satisfied when His sons and daughters dwell together in unity, accomplishing His will. One of Egypt's gifts to the nations is to reconcile families. It's the land where dreams are fulfilled, but without family, dreams mean nothing.

Out of Egypt, God called His firstborn to Himself...as a people of worship, a kingdom of priests.

Chapter 8
Egypt: Where Worship Begins
God's Deliverer

Generations passed and Joseph's legacy began to fade in the hearts of the Egyptians and their Pharaohs. Instead of seeing Joseph's family as a blessing, they concluded that this multitude of Hebrew descendants was a threat to national security. So, what do you do with a developing minority? You oppress them, control their birth rate, deny them good jobs and education, force them to stay in their poor slums and silence their voices lest they revolt and overturn your government. That's exactly what Pharaoh did: he enslaved the Hebrews and when they raised their voices, they were given harsh masters to double their work. Not only that, but Pharaoh also issued a law legalising infanticide, killing newly born Hebrew boys.[29]

It was in this political landscape that Moses was born. According to Pharaoh, Moses' little body was destined to be breakfast for the Nile crocodiles. But God's purposes for this baby overruled Pharaoh's decree. The book of Exodus starts with a cry, not in revolt against Pharaoh, but an appeal to God:

"The children of Israel groaned because of the bondage and they cried out... So, God heard their groaning and God remembered His covenant with Abraham, with Isaac and with Jacob and God looked upon the children of Israel and God acknowledged them." (Exodus 2:23-25)

The Birth of the deliverer

When Moses was born, his parents decided to defy Pharaoh's policy. Like all the other boys being born, baby Moses was also thrown into the Nile but concealed in a basket. His little boat floated downstream and stopped at the feet of Pharaoh's daughter. When she opened the basket and saw what was in it, she recognised that the baby was Hebrew and with a softened heart, she decided to adopt him.

Thus, Moses grew up in the royal courts of Egypt. Undoubtedly, he learned the Egyptian traditions, culture, language and (most likely) the pagan idol worship. The Bible doesn't tell us anything about this season of his life, but we must assume that the Egyptian ways were deeply engraved into his soul. We do not know when or how he came to know the God of Abraham, Isaac and Jacob, but we do know that God was working on his heart and that his soul was wrestling. We get a glimpse of this when his zeal for justice is aroused upon seeing one of his Hebrew brothers being beaten by an Egyptian man. Moses goes into full rage and kills the Egyptian and hides him in the sand. When word gets out, Moses realises that he is in big trouble. Perhaps there was a way to appease Pharaoh and explain what happened? Undoubtedly, he seriously wrestled over this. The book of Hebrews shines a light on his internal dialogue.

"By faith Moses, when he became of age, refused to be called the son of Pharaoh's daughter, choosing rather to suffer affliction with the people of God than to enjoy the passing pleasures of sin, esteeming the reproach of Christ greater riches than the treasures in Egypt; for he looked to the reward. By faith he forsook Egypt, not fearing the wrath of the king; for he endured as seeing Him who is invisible." (Hebrews 11: 24-27)

The Land of Midian

Moses made his choice to walk away from his right to royal privilege, becoming a fugitive and running all the way to the land of Midian. This region, located near the Red Sea in the western deserts of modern-day Saudi Arabia, is where Moses found not only refuge, but a wife named Zipporah, a daughter of the priest of Midian. At the well, where Moses met her, his destiny was starting to be realised. (Exodus 2:15-21) If you recall, it was the Ishmaelite traders from the land of Midian who brought Joseph to Egypt.[30] Now, generations later, Moses finds himself among those same people, his distant cousins! One day, as Moses was tending sheep in Midian, he saw a bush that was on fire, but it was not being consumed. Immediately, the Angel of the Lord spoke to him from within the bush. The pre-incarnate Christ, who once encountered Hagar and Ishmael, was now seeking Moses out, instructing him on how to deliver His people. (Exodus 3)

Why didn't God encounter Moses anywhere else along the way? Why did he wait for him to settle in Midian? I believe God wanted to meet him among family. He intended that the family of Ishmael and Midian be witnesses and partakers of what was about to take place. After all, it was because of them that Moses' ancestors were brought into Egypt. God was being faithful to His promise to Abraham and honouring all his children, bringing them back together, full circle, continuing to fulfil their family destiny. God was calling Moses to go back to Egypt and tell Pharoah to "let His people go." (Exodus 4:22-23)

God gave Moses a sign of His commitment to this assignment: Moses would bring the people back to that very mountain, in the land of Midian, to worship Him. (Exodus 3:12) Moses, recognising the holiness of this encounter, takes off his shoes and reluctantly agrees to the impossible mission ahead of him.

Let my people worship me

One of the main reasons God was bringing His people out of Egypt was for the purpose of worship. For generations they were under a system of demonic worship. Now, God was calling them to Himself, to come out of Egypt, to give themselves purely to worship Him. He would establish them as a kingdom of priests. In the process, God would confront the old system, revealing the new.

Confronting fake worship

Egypt had one of the most organised and intricate forms of idol worship in the ancient world. When you go to visit the temples of Egypt today, you notice the design is very similar to Moses' tabernacle and Solomon's temple, starting with the outer court, leading to the holy place and then the inmost part, the holy of holies. Is this a coincidence or a copy? Which one is the original?

Historically speaking, Egypt was already established as a nation of worship before the arrival of Joseph and his family. The temples, the idols, the priesthood and the sacrifices were all in operation. Those temples were built much earlier than Moses' tabernacle and Solomon's temple. So, did Moses copy what he had seen in Egypt, then Solomon followed suit? Scripture tells us that God showed Moses the heavenly design, according to which he would build the tabernacle. (Exodus 25:9, Hebrews 8:5)

So, how did ancient Egypt come up with a similar design? We know that Lucifer had access to the throne room of God, he knew heaven's form of worship. When his heart was exalted, desiring that worship to himself, he fell. I believe that he influenced the Egyptian Empire (and all pagan worship for that matter) to build its worship system as a twisted copy of the heavenly pattern. In this, he would receive the worship that people offered the idols he inspired, standing in competition and total rebellion to the One who sits on the throne.[31] I recently visited a temple in Luxor and I couldn't help but think of the intense demonic spiritual atmosphere that must have been present in those days. What was it like for Moses and Aaron to walk into these ancient courts challenging their gods? Moses, having just encountered the God of heaven and earth, was filled with courage and boldness to walk right past the priests, the sacrifices and demonic practices and to go face to face with Pharaoh, confronting the gods of Egypt, against whom God was planning to execute judgment.(Exodus 12:12)

Yahweh, the hidden name revealed

When God sent Moses as deliverer, it was crucial that he was fully equipped. The confrontation that Moses was about to encounter, was going to be fierce, he needed God to manifest himself on his behalf. He needed God to declare His name. God did.

"I am the Lord. I appeared to Abraham, to Isaac and to Jacob as God Almighty, but by my name the Lord (Yahweh) I did not make myself fully known to them ... Therefore, say to the Israelites: 'I am the Lord, and I will bring you out from under the yoke of the Egyptians...' Then you will know that I am the Lord your God, who brought you out from under the yoke of the Egyptians." (Exodus 6:2-7)

Up to this time, God was not known to his people as Yahweh.[32] It was crucial now for Him to unveil His identity, because it was directly connected to the victory He was about to release. His name reflects His nature. The revelation of the nature of God is vital in our spiritual warfare so we can walk in victory.

As Pharaoh's heart hardened against the Lord, Moses released a series of plagues, one after another. God declared the power and authority of His name, confronting the fake system of worship and causing even the magicians who failed to copy Moses' wonders to confess "this is the finger of God." (Exodus 8:18-19)

Before the coming of the Lord, there is going to be a spiritual confrontation much fiercer than what Moses experienced. Jesus said that the plagues which the world will endure will be much harder, more widespread and more devastating. (Matthew 24:21) But God is preparing His bride to challenge, confront and overcome the kingdoms of the world. How will we overcome? Through the revelation of the new name.

"Now I saw heaven opened and behold, a white horse. And He who sat on him was called Faithful and True and in righteousness He judges and makes war. His eyes were like a flame of fire and on His head were many crowns. He had a name written that no one knew except Himself." (Revelation 19:11:12)

This new name is concealed now, but I believe it will be revealed to the generation that will need to use the power of that name. We currently have all we need to overcome the power of darkness, but God is about to manifest himself as never before. Just as in the days of Moses—when never before had a sea split in two, the sky rained down food, a river come out of a rock, nor every firstborn of an entire nation be killed in one day—God will again reveal His nature in a great and a terrible way to crush the works of darkness once and for all. (Revelation 12:10-12)

The Revelation of the Lamb

"Who is the Lord that I should obey his voice to let Israel go. I do not know the Lord, nor will I let Israel go." (Exodus 5:2)

These were Pharaoh's words when Moses appeared before him. Now, nine plagues had passed, causing the destruction of Egypt's economy and infrastructure, yet

Pharaoh's heart was still hardened; hence, God gave Pharaoh the final ultimatum.

"Thus says the Lord, 'Israel is my son, my first born, so I say to you, let my son go so he may serve me; but if you refuse to let him go, indeed I will kill your son, your first born.'" (Exodus 4:23)

As He was preparing to deal this final blow to Egypt, God gave Moses instructions to observe the Passover. It was in Egypt that a corporate revelation of the Lamb of God was first unveiled to God's people. On Egyptian soil, the blood of thousands of lambs was spilled as the first communion service ever to take place in history occurred as the passover meal was celebrated. It was all pointing to a future Passover Day when the Son of God, the pure and spotless Lamb, would be slain for the sins of the world. In Egypt, the blood was put on the doorposts and when the Angel of death saw it, he passed over and spared whoever was hidden under the shelter of the blood.

"For I will pass through the land of Egypt and will strike all the first born in the land of Egypt ... and against all the gods of Egypt I will execute judgment. I AM THE LORD ... when I see the blood, I will pass over you." (Exodus 12:12)

This was an act of judgment and mercy at the same time. The decisive factor of which side one experienced weighed on the choice to humbly obey. This atoning work was sufficient not only for God's people, but also for any Egyptian or other Gentile who believed and trusted in His name. So any "stranger" who would comply with the command of circumcision and observe the Passover, would be "as a native of the land." (Exodus 12:48, 49) But for all those, including Pharaoh, who didn't heed the warnings, devastation awaited.

"Pharaoh rose in the night, he, all his servants and all the Egyptians; and there was a great cry in Egypt. For there was not a house where there was not one dead." (Exodus 12:30)

What was the cry in that day like? I wonder what implication that painful wound has had on subsequent generations of Egyptians? I wonder if there has ever been a national healing of that cry in the heart of Egypt? Is there a poetic symmetry in that similar cries arose from the mothers in Bethlehem when Herod's decree went forth seeking to kill baby Jesus? Perhaps His very presence, as a child taking refuge in Egypt, deposited a seed of healing in the land. These are questions in my heart, but we can be certain that, according to the words of Isaiah, God heals when he strikes: He will fully restore "His people" Egypt.

"Then the Lord will be known to Egypt, the Egyptians will know the Lord in that day and will make sacrifice and offering; yes, they will make a vow to the Lord and perform it. And the Lord will strike Egypt, He will strike and heal it; they will return to the Lord, and He will be entreated by them and heal them." (Isaiah 19:21,22, 24)

The first worship sanctuary at the foot of the mountain

God delivered His people with His mighty hand and outstretched arm as they crossed the Red Sea, pursued by Pharaoh and his chariots. The Lord closed the sea, killing the Egyptian army; in so doing, He was issuing his people a one-way ticket on their journey to become a nation of worshippers. Just as He had said, God led them to the mountain of Horeb in the land of Midian, where He had initially met Moses. (Exodus 3:12)

The Tabernacle of Moses was established at the foot of that mountain, but where did the Israelites get materials to build the tabernacle? Remember, their Egyptian neighbours gave them gold, silver and clothing as they exited. This first worship sanctuary was built with the gold of Egypt! (Exodus 3:22)

For the first time in the history of this new nation, there was a priesthood. It came from the tribe of Levi (Levites), commissioned to carry the Tabernacle from place to place, erecting it according to the instruction of the Lord. Every time they settled; the twelve tribes would be situated around it with the tribe of Judah at the main entrance. The Ark of the covenant was situated in the most holy place and the golden lamp stand and the articles of the tabernacle were handmade, according to the divine pattern. When they finally arrived at the promised land, the "Ark of the covenant of the Lord of all the earth" made with Egyptian gold, crossed the flooding Jordan on the shoulders of the priests, leading the people into their destiny (Joshua 3:11). Out of Egypt, God called His firstborn to Himself, using the wealth of Egypt to equip and establish them as a people of worship, a kingdom of priests.

Where is the Mountain of God?

Throughout modern Christian history it has been thought that Mount Sinai rests in Egypt's Sinai Peninsula. (It is disputed as to whether the mountain received its name from the region, or the region was named after the mountain.)[33] If it lies in the land of ancient Midian, however, then this mountain could lie somewhere in Saudi Arabia, and not in Sinai-Egypt, as has long been the belief.

There have been a lot of recent archeological hypotheses proposed to support this view.[34] As I am writing this chapter, I am literally camping at the foot of that very mountain; I am in awe at what took place three thousand years ago. It is fascinating how these sights accurately reflect the biblical record and it's beautiful to encounter the Lord at the site of the burning bush! Paul, writing to the Galatians, refers to this mountain as "Mount Sinai in Arabia." (Galatians 4:25)

Paul, a pharisee who thoroughly knew the Scriptures, was on a crusade to stamp out the growing following of Jesus, persecuting Christians to protect the Law of Moses. But after a personal encounter with Jesus in Damascus, Paul went to Arabia for a period of three years, where he records that Jesus Christ taught him the gospel. (Galations 1:11-17) Is it possible that Paul, in search of the true meaning of the law, intentionally went to "Mount Sinai in Arabia" where the law was originally given? I believe that he did. It was there that Paul finally understood that the Christ had come and was the very fulfilment of the Law and the Prophets.

That time in Arabia transformed Paul's life with the revelation needed to pen a large portion of the New Testament! Paradoxically, six centuries later, not too far from that mountain, another man had another encounter from another spirit, instructing him to start a new religion that would deny the sonship of Christ and the Fatherhood of God! [35]

Perhaps the turning of attention toward this mountain in Saudi Arabia in our generation is a tremendous sign from heaven. The God of the burning bush that appeared to Moses, the same God that revealed the Messiah to Paul, is the God that is ready to reveal His nature to millions of the sons of Ishmael in the very heart of the Muslim world! Abraham's and Hagar's prayers for Ishmael still echo in the courts of heaven: "May Ishmael live before you." These prayers are still being answered in our lifetime.

A new worship calendar

"And it came to pass at the end of the four hundred and thirty years—on that very same day [the Passover and final plague of death]—it came to pass that all the armies of the Lord went out from the land of Egypt. It is a night of solemn observance to the Lord for bringing them out of the land of Egypt." (Exodus 12:41, 42)

This was the day Israel was born—the most important day in her history. This was the day where redemption was manifested and guaranteed for all future generations. This day was so special that God decided to initiate a whole new calendar to commemorate it. "This month shall be your beginning of months. It shall be the first month of the year." (Exodus 12:2) This new Hebrew calendar, marking the record of Biblical history from that moment onward, was instituted in Egypt. The people of God needed to separate themselves from the Egyptian calendar and from the Egyptian system of worship; they needed to join themselves to the heavenly calendar that reflects God's ways, times and seasons. His people not only needed to come out physically, but their whole orientation and the rhythms of life needed to be shifted. Following Yahweh meant detachment from the system of the world, letting go of the old mindsets and tuning in to the heartbeat of heaven.

As He brought them out of Egypt, a land full of pagan worship, God was birthing Israel as a nation of heavenly worship. This would be their new identity before God. Therefore, it was necessary that He gave them a new calendar to reflect the seasons of sowing, feasting and resting to remember His goodness and worship Him accordingly. If you have read the end of God's story, you have learned that there is a time coming when God will once again initiate a new calendar: a Millennial one. When Christ, our Passover Lamb slain before the foundations of the world, comes again, as the "Greater Moses" (Hebrews 3:3), he will deliver the earth from the "pharaohs" of this age[36] and all works of darkness. He will set His throne in Jerusalem and birth a new phase of history, as He did on the first Passover.

The Bible says that in that day, Egypt will be restored to her true identity as a nation of worship, but not unto false gods; rather, unto the Holy One of Israel. There will be a worship movement arising from the heart of Egypt, reaching out to all the surrounding nations, even unto

Iran, joining with the people of God in Israel, together becoming a blessing to all the earth. (Isaiah 19:23,24) Across the globe, even to the farthest Islands, every soul, seeing His worth, His justice and victory, will bow in worship and every tongue will confess that He is the Lord —all will join the heavenly chorus, singing to the Lamb:

"You are worthy to take the scroll and to open its seals; for you were slain and have redeemed us to God by your blood out of every tribe and tongue and people and nation and have made us kings and priests to our God; And we shall reign on the earth." (Revelation 5:9,10)

SHADI

Section 3
God's Handiwork

MENE MENE: God Has Numbered Your Kingdom and Finished It;

TEKEL: You Have Been Weighed in the Balances, and Found Wanting;

UPHARSIN: Your Kingdom Has Been Divided and Given to the Medes and Persians .
(Daniel 5:25-28)

These words mark the shifting of kingdoms and a historical transition that forever changed the world: the rise of the Persians, a global superpower for the next few hundred years.

While Egypt was clearly portrayed as the womb for the nation of Israel, providing a historical backdrop for the preservation of the Messianic bloodline and the forging of a covenant nation of priests and prophets. Babylon and Persia (the region of Assyria) were the fertile seedbed for clarity of future promises. Even amid constant threats of a total annihilation of Jerusalem, her people and her temple, this era and region served as a greenhouse, preserving and cultivating growth of the nation. Here, Ezekiel, Daniel and Zechariah received prophetic understanding about God's redemptive plan for the Isaiah 19 nations.

In this section, we will explore the role of Persia and her kings as it relates to Israel and how it connects with Egypt. To understand this, it is important to lay a foundation of historical context for the coming chapters.

SHADI

Chapter 9
A Historical Bridge

Reading through the biblical accounts of the historical events from this point in our journey, things may not be so clearly deciphered at first glance. When sorting through the chronology, terms/names for identifying various historical persons and varying perspectives found in the accounts, there appears to be some gaps left when trying to see how all the data-points connect. There are a few clarifying details I discovered as I was on my personal journey of understanding that I want to share here, combining others' biblical scholarship with various historical and extra-biblical references.

Israel: from promise to exile

Following the Exodus, Moses led the people of Israel out of Egypt with a great display of power. But the new nation wandered for forty years, not readily trusting the God who had delivered them. Under the leadership of Joshua, the next generation finally crossed over to possess the land of promise, experiencing great exploits and challenges; however, this generation did not retain the wonder and awe of God. Israel was bent toward rebellion and after Joshua's death, the people were ruled by judges for centuries[37]. These judges were raised up to deliver Israel time and time again. Eventually, they insisted upon having a king like the surrounding nations.

God responded to their hearts' desire and appointed Saul from the tribe of Benjamin to be the first King of Israel. He was removed from the throne after his heart hardened in rebellion and David became the newly anointed king, ruling over the twelve tribes. David was a man after God's heart. After building the tabernacle of worship, he made it a primary goal to build the temple to honour the Lord. God didn't allow David to build the temple, promising that his son would, also promising to retain his descendants' place on the throne.

Solomon was the next to reign over the whole nation. He built the glorious temple for Yahweh, fulfilling the desire that had been in David's heart. Unfortunately, despite the great favour of God in his life, Solomon's heart hardened toward the Lord. Consequently, the kingdom was divided (1 Kings 11:31-35) and the tribes of Judah and Benjamin became the Southern Kingdom (Judah), while the Northern Kingdom (Israel) was composed of the other ten tribes.

The temple in Jerusalem remained the primary centre of worship in the southern kingdom, but the northern kingdom erected altars to worship the idols it had adopted. Except for short periods throughout their subsequent history, both the northern and southern kingdoms eventually wandered completely from the ways of Yahweh.

The Lord in His mercy, sent prophetic messengers, such as Isaiah and Jeremiah, to call Israel to repentance, but to no avail. Ultimately, the Lord gave them a final warning: if they refused to repent and return, they would become captives, losing nation and land. The northern kingdom was eventually taken captive by Assyria, which dispersed the ten tribes throughout the Assyrian Empire. The southern kingdom was eventually taken over by the Babylonians. It is here that we take up the story of how Israel [38] was preserved.[39]

The Babylonians

Under the leadership of Nebuchadnezzar, Babylon continued to expand its holdings, finally acquiring the coveted land of Israel. According to many scholars, the story of the Babylonian captivity is complex. In the first of the three waves of captivity (c.605BC), the Babylonians extracted all the attractive nobility of high status and royal blood, including Daniel and his now famous friends. (Daniel 1) This followed with a more aggressive occupation of the capital city in 597BC—the final fall of Jerusalem occurred in 586BC. The entire city, including the temple, was looted and destroyed, with a vassal governor, Gedeliah, left to maintain Babylon's authority in the area. [40]

God then raised up Nebuchadnezzar,[41] but as his haughtiness grew, God humbled him until he was able to recognise that there is a God in heaven who rules over the affairs of all men. (Daniel 4:34,35) His successor, Belshazzar, did not learn from his humiliation. Demonstrating his gaul, Belshazzar brought the consecrated articles that were taken from the temple in Jerusalem and used them dishonorably, for his own feasting. Immediately, God confronted him. A hand appeared on the wall, writing a sentence that terrified the King and his aides: "Mene Mene Tekel and Upharsim." They immediately looked for someone to explain the phrase. Daniel, a Jewish scholar in the court of the kings of Babylon, now in his eighties, was brought before Belshazzar and not only translated the message, but authoritatively declared that this king and his kingdom had been weighed (by God) and found shorthanded. Therefore, the kingdom would be given over to the Persians and the Medes. (Daniel 5)

The walls of Babylon were believed to be impregnable, as the massive city was surrounded by water from the Euphrates River. While the people inside the palace were intoxicated and using the holy articles from the temple of God in their festivities, they were oblivious to what was happening around the city walls outside the palace, as the Persian army was executing a plan that would bring the city down.

In one of the earliest accounts of Babylon's capture, outside of the Biblical record, the Greek historian Herodotus alludes to the Persian army's plan to enter the city underneath the walls overnight, for a surprise take-over of the city.[42] While other scholars since Herodotus have proposed differing scenarios for the takeover, we know that King Belshazzar was overcome, as Daniel had prophesied. Thus, the Babylonians' fall was a major steppingstone for the Medo-Persians' epic rise to world power, under Cyrus the Great, opening a new chapter for the future of Israel. (Daniel 5:30,31)

The Medo-Persian Empire

It is helpful to note that Daniel received and recorded understanding about the Medo-Persian Empire in two visions in Daniel 7:5, 8:1-4,20. In the first, he saw an image of a bear tilted on one side, which is understood by most scholars to be the Medo-Persian Empire.[43] In chapter eight, Daniel records another vision of a ram with two horns and indicates that an angel gives him the interpretation of this figure as representing the rise of a Medo-Persian Empire.[44]

Thus, the Medo-Persian Empire, in becoming the dominant world power for the next two-hundred years (until the rise of the Greeks), subjugating the Jews, among other peoples, was clearly positioned by God on the stage of history to accomplish His purposes for Israel and the nations.

Cyrus and Darius: Connecting the dots

The books of Daniel, Haggai, Zechariah, Ezra, Nehemiah, Esther and Malachi were all written in the Persian era, giving glimpses of what was happening with the people of Israel in this time. Seeing the timeline woven through these books is key to seeing the hand of God orchestrating His purposes through this period of history.

Throughout the biblical writings from this era, the names used for the Persian rulers can, at times, be confusing as there are multiple generations of leaders sharing the same names: Cyrus I, II, Darius I, II, III, Xerxes, Artaxerxes, etc. To further muddy the situation, the Persian Kings are also referenced by other names in various external historical records: Greek, Assyrian, Roman, etc. The goal of this section is to not get lost in scholarly jargon or debates around the textual discrepancies, but to keep our focus on the storyline.

Throughout the coming chapters, I will bring us into a focus on the events that happen in the first year of Cyrus's reign. It is precisely here to which many historical and theological discussions and theories are directed.

In Daniel 5:31-6:1 and 6:28, Daniel refers to the first year of the reign of "Darius the Mede" and then also that of Cyrus. Then in chapter 9:1 and 11:1, he refers, again, to the reign of "Darius the Mede". (There are several Persian kings named Darius, but they come on the scene much later than Daniel's lifetime, so we know he is not referring to any of those kings.)

Some use these texts to discredit the entire book of Daniel, while others propose varying possibilities for reconciling Daniel's writings with archeology sources.[45] The most helpful resource I have found is a recent doctoral dissertation, written by Dr Steven Anderson (Dallas Theological Seminary), in which he clearly lays out the various historical views and evidences, connecting the dots congruently with the idea of Cyrus having a co-regent for at least an early portion of his rule over this new territory.[46] This actually resonates with the speculations of previous historians that "Darius the Mede" could have been appointed by Cyrus to transition the Babylonian government of Nebuchadnezzar to Cyrus's rule.[47]

So, in highlighting the significance of Cyrus in God's plan in the coming chapters, I will build on the foundation of this persuasion that Daniel's references to the first year of "Darius the Mede" are simultaneously referring to the first year of Cyrus the Great.

This clarity about Darius "the Mede" helps to avoid confusing Daniel's references (mentioned above) with Darius I (522BC-486BC) or Darius II (423BC-405BC), who later ruled the dynasty. In his classic work, 'The History of the Persian Empire', A.T. Olmstead provides detailed accounts of the events surrounding Darius I's accession to the throne. Corroborated by modern research, it is thought that Cyrus died while expanding his Empire (around 523BC) and his son, Cambyses II (identified in Ezra 4:6 as Ahasuerus or Akhshurosh), was conquering the remaining territory of Egypt for Persia.[48] However, Cambyses's rule was not long lived, as he never returned to Babylon to take the throne. It is thought that the throne was stolen for a short time by a usurper (Bardiya or Smerdis), but this illegitimate ascent to the throne was cut short as Darius I, the former spear-bearer of Cyrus the Great, claimed the right to lead Persia.[49] It is plausible that because Darius I was married to the daughter of Cyrus (sister of Cambyses), he was able to maintain the trust of the Persian army and thus claim the throne, furthering the glory of the Empire within the plans and purposes of God.

Waves of return

The Jews' captivity took place in three waves and it is interesting to see that their return to their homeland also occurred in three waves. The first was initiated in the first year of the reign of Cyrus the Great (536BC) and was primarily led by Zerubbabel and Joshua the high priest. (Ezra 1, 2)

Within the book of Ezra, the first six chapters recall the historical events some eighty years before the accounts of the last four chapters. It is Darius I, in Ezra 6, who recalls the decree of Cyrus to return the Jews to their homeland and so reaffirms their efforts to continue rebuilding their temple in Jerusalem (under Zerubbabel).

Furthermore, the story recorded in the book of Esther takes place between the last verses of Ezra 6 and the first verse of Ezra 7. So, this one verse gap is likely to span over five decades[50]. It is helpful to see that in total, Ezra covers a period of almost ninety years.

Scripture says that the Persian king Artaxerxes, grandson of Darius I (referenced above), commissioned Ezra to lead a delegation back in (458BC-second wave) and then later (444BC-third wave) gave Nehemiah permission to return to rebuild Jerusalem.[51] [52]

The following timeline serves to both bridge any gaps and trace the theme of God's plan as it relates to the people of Israel in the Persian context.[53] With the complex historical framework in place, we can look more deeply at the importance of Iran's predecessors in shaping the people and nation of Israel.[54]

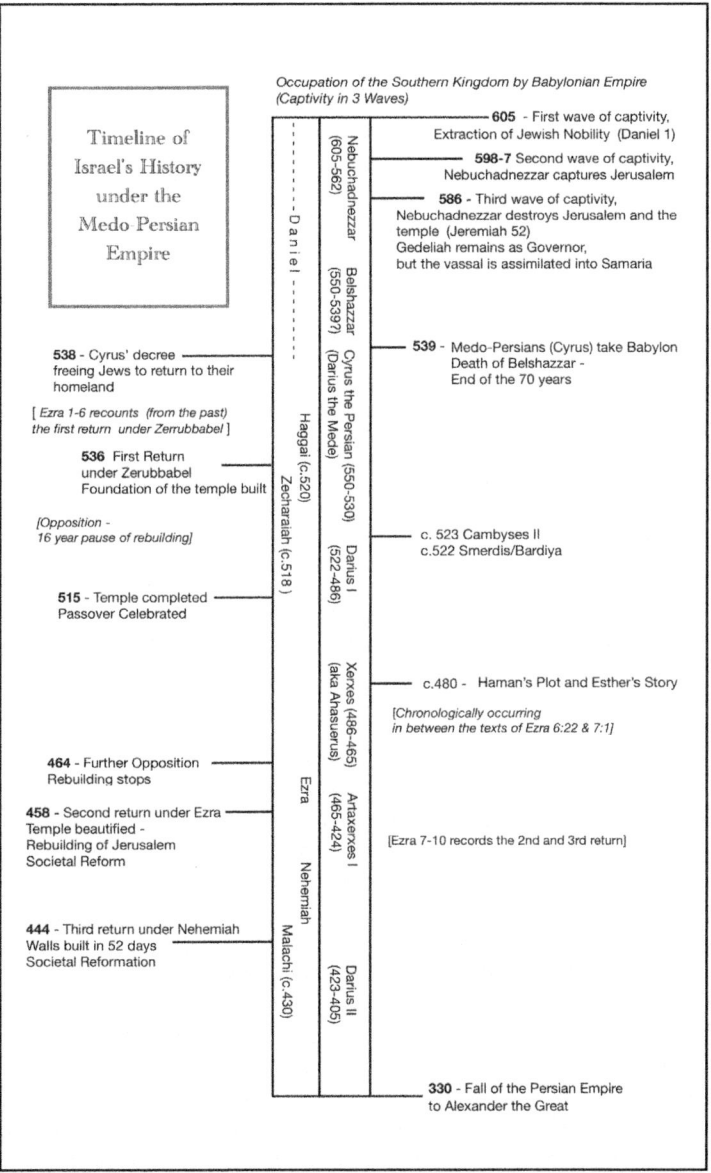

Timeline of
Israel's History
under the
Medo Persian
Empire

Occupation of the Southern Kingdom by Babylonian Empire
(Captivity in 3 Waves)

Daniel

Nebuchadnezzar (605-562)

605 - First wave of captivity,
Extraction of Jewish Nobility (Daniel 1)

598-7 Second wave of captivity,
Nebuchadnezzar captures Jerusalem

586 - Third wave of captivity,
Nebuchadnezzar destroys Jerusalem and the
temple (Jeremiah 52)
Gedeliah remains as Governor,
but the vassal is assimilated into Samaria

Belshazzar (550-539?)

538 - Cyrus' decree
freeing Jews to return to their
homeland

[Ezra 1-6 recounts (from the past)
the first return under Zerrubbabel]

Cyrus the Persian (550-530)
(Darius the Mede)

539 - Medo-Persians (Cyrus) take Babylon
Death of Belshazzar -
End of the 70 years

Haggai (c.520)

536 First Return
under Zerubbabel
Foundation of the temple built

Zechariah (c.518)

[Opposition -
16 year pause of rebuilding]

Darius I (522-486)

c. 523 Cambyses II
c.522 Smerdis/Bardiya

515 - Temple completed
Passover Celebrated

Xerxes (486-465)
(aka Ahasuerus)

c.480 - Haman's Plot and Esther's Story

[Chronologically occurring
in between the texts of Ezra 6:22 & 7:1]

464 - Further Opposition
Rebuilding stops

Ezra

458 - Second return under Ezra
Temple beautified -
Rebuilding of Jerusalem
Societal Reform

Artaxerxes I (465-424)

[Ezra 7-10 records the 2nd and 3rd return]

Nehemiah

444 - Third return under Nehemiah
Walls built in 52 days
Societal Reformation

Malachi (c.430)

Darius II (423-405)

330 - Fall of the Persian Empire
to Alexander the Great

God is not a "respecter of persons." (Acts 10:34-35) He can accomplish His plans through anyone.

Chapter 10

Iran: Where Freedom Is Granted

God's Anointed

"Whenever you can, act as a liberator. Freedom, dignity, wealth - these three together constitute the greatest happiness of humanity. If you bequeath all three to your people, their love for you will never die."[55]
(Cyrus the Great)

Cyrus the Great, founder of the Medo-Persian (aka Achaemenid) Empire, built his Empire through extensive military conquest, taking the Median, Lydian and Babylonian kingdoms. His kingdom spanned over two million square miles, stretching from the Aegean Sea to southwestern Asia and reaching to the southern portions of Egypt to parts of Greece and then east to parts of India. [56] He stands out in history as a different breed of ruler, establishing a kingdom that was tolerant to different people groups; able to pacify new territories; giving economic and social opportunities to exiles; honouring people's different faiths; and in many cases encouraging the return of exiles to their homeland.[57]

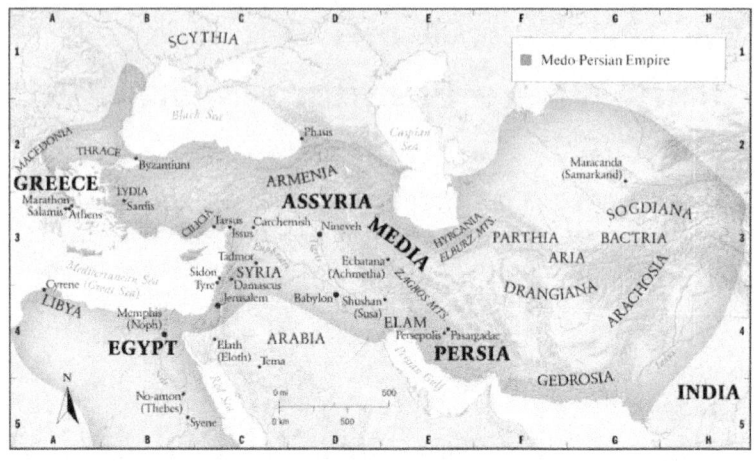

The Medo-Persian Empire (Image source: Andrews)

The Cyrus Cylinder

In 1879, the Cyrus Cylinder was discovered in Babylon, Iraq. A baked clay cylinder in the Akkadian language with cuneiform script, the artefact contains one of the earliest written records of an official government's declaration of human rights. Inscribed on it are the records indicating that Cyrus freed slaves, declared that all people had the right to choose their own religion and established racial equality. This ancient historical record matches the biblical record of the return of the exiles. It has been noted that the contents of this decree harmonise with the modern Universal Declaration of Human Rights, drafted and proclaimed by the United Nations in 1948. [58]

The Cyrus Cylinder currently sits in the British Museum in London - (Photo by Author 2015)

The biblical Cyrus

Though Cyrus was an idol-worshipping gentile king seeking to build an Empire for his own namesake, God anointed him for His purposes and called him by name from the mouth of the prophet Isaiah almost two hundred years before his birth.

"Thus says the Lord to His anointed, To Cyrus, whose right hand I have held—To subdue nations before him and loose the armour of kings, to open before him the double doors, so that the gates will not be shut: 'I will go before you and make the crooked places straight; I will break in pieces the gates of bronze and cut the bars of iron. I will give you the treasures of darkness and hidden riches of secret places,that you may know that I, the Lord, who call you by your name, am the God of Israel. For Jacob My servant's sake and Israel My elect, I have even called you by your name; I have named you, though you have not known Me. I am the Lord and there is no other; there is no God besides Me. I will gird you, though you have not known Me, that they may know from the rising of the sun to its setting that there is none besides Me. I am the Lord, and there is no other." (Isaiah 45:1-7)

God spoke about this Persian man far before his lifetime, far ahead of the captivity itself. God knew that His people would one day be under the hand of Cyrus following seventy years of captivity under another king, and he would literally shepherd them into a season of rebuilding.

"The Lord who says of Cyrus, 'He is My shepherd, and he shall perform all My pleasure,' saying to Jerusalem, 'You shall be built,' and to the temple, 'Your foundation shall be laid.'" (Isaiah 44:26-28)

Though his rule is clearly referred to in the biblical texts,[59] it seems that Cyrus was most occupied elsewhere in his empire and not so present in Babylon. Nevertheless, it is probable that Cyrus knew about Isaiah's prophecies, referring to him by name; as the historian Josephus wrote; "When Cyrus read this [writing of Isaiah] and admired the divine power, an earnest desire and an ambition seized upon him, to fulfil what was so written." [60]

In the previous chapter, I addressed in more detail a specific question of the historical Cyrus in the biblical context. To summarise the issue, Daniel refers to the incoming Medo-Persian ruler by two different names: Darius the Mede and Cyrus. (Daniel 5:31-6:1; 6:28; 9:1; 11:1) Though some modern historians use this seeming discrepancy to discredit the entire book of Daniel, I am not convinced that this indicates a contradiction, but rather an indication Daniel could be referring to two men ruling in the same time period in different capacities, as Cyrus was securing loyalty in the newly acquired Babylonian territory. [61]

Regardless of how one interprets the evidence available, now or in the future, we know that God is not a "respecter of persons." (Acts 10:34-35) He can accomplish His plans through anyone. God knows the end from the beginning. He raises up kings just at the right time to accomplish His plans and purposes. He shifts kingdom and empires for the sole purpose of moving His agenda forward. Kingdoms come and kingdoms go but the kingdom of God will remain forever.

So, what was the will of God in choosing and anointing Cyrus to release His captives, the Jews? According to Isaiah, God was anointing this man for the sake of Israel, giving him a clear mandate to rebuild Jerusalem and lay down the foundations of the temple.

The rule of Cyrus the Great inspired many significant strides in the history of human rights and religious freedom.[62] In light of this rich heritage, I cannot help but ponder Iran's current human rights situation now (2023). We have recently seen unprecedented protests in Iran, with thousands gathering in Tehran's largest square "ميدان آزادی, - Meydane Azadi" (translated Freedom Square), protesting their government's harsh controls, willing to die as they are ready to fight for their own freedoms. Many of our brothers and sisters in Christ suffer daily under this regime.[63]

We pray for the people of Iran today, that the Lord will bring true freedom to their nation through the knowledge of God's unconditional love, displayed through His Son, who alone can set them free.

ISRAEL, BORN IN EGYPT, RAISED IN IRAN

...It is those small steps of disciplining our flesh today that prepares us to be steadfast and unwavering tomorrow. The battle is overcome in the belly before it's overcome in the den.

Chapter 11

Iran: Where the Battle Is Fought

God's Intercessor

"A theology of hope must be rooted in the belief that God is who He says He is and that He, knowing the end from the beginning, is involved in human history from beginning to end."[64] [65]

(R. Corrie)

There are moments in history that are assigned by God to shift nations and to advance His eternal purposes. He moves His purposes forward through men and women who choose to submit to His leadership, responding accordingly to His perfect wisdom and timing. The first year that Cyrus became king of Persia was a key moment that shifted history, a convergence of God's appointed time with willing hearts on the earth. Cyrus, his vassal Darius,[66] and Daniel were anointed by God to see heaven's plans connect to reality on earth in their generation. The book of Daniel records several key events that occurred in the first year of the reign of Cyrus/Darius:

1. The fulfilment of Jeremiah's prophecy ending seventy years of exile. (Daniel 9:1-2)

2. The Medo-Persian Empire overtakes the Babylonian Empire. (Daniel 5:30-31)

3. The archangels Gabriel and Michael fight against the prince of Persia. (Daniel 11:1)

4. Daniel is thrown in the lions' den. (Daniel 5:30-6:16)

5. Cyrus issues a decree freeing the Jewish exiles. (Ezra 1:1-4; 2 Chronicles 36:22,23)

6. The fulfilment of Isaiah's prophecy concerning Cyrus. (Isaiah 44-45)

It is important to ask some questions here: Were these simply random and unrelated events that happened to occur in the same year? Or were they somehow connected and perhaps even consequential? If so, what was the main event that set everything in motion?

I would like to suggest that the first event that had a dynamic domino effect was Daniel's prayer, recorded in Daniel 9: "In the first year of Darius, the son of Ahasuerus, of the lineage of the Medes who was made king over the realm of the Chaldeans, in the first year of his reign, I Daniel understood by the books, the number of years specified by the word of the Lord through Jeremiah the prophet, (Jeremiah 25:9-14; 29:10-14) that He would accomplish seventy years in the desolation of Jerusalem." (Daniel 9:1-2)

He is referring to the writing of Jeremiah: "After seventy years are completed at Babylon, I (the Lord) will visit you and perform My good word toward you and cause you to return to this place. For I know the thoughts that I think toward you, says the Lord, thoughts of peace and not of evil, to give you a future and a hope ... I will be found by you; says the Lord and I will bring you back from your captivity." (Jeremiah 29:10-14)

Undoubtedly, Daniel was also familiar with Isaiah's prophecy about Cyrus (detailed in the last chapter), uttered two hundred years before. While the exact dates are not clear, Cyrus suddenly becomes the new king around the time of the seventieth year of the exile.

The convergence of the prophetic words of Isaiah and Jeremiah, in time and space, caused Daniel to recognise the divine and historic moment in which he was living. When Daniel realises that the time has come for the fulfilment of these prophecies, his response (to God and to His word) is to set his face toward Jerusalem and toward the Lord in prayer, fasting and repentance: "Cause Your face to shine on Your sanctuary, which is desolate. Oh my God, incline your ear and hear; open your eyes and see our desolations ... Oh Lord, hear! Oh Lord, forgive! Oh Lord, listen and act! Do not delay for Your own sake, my God, for Your city and Your people are called by Your name." (Daniel 9:17b-19) Daniel's prayer was catalytic; it triggered a reaction in the spirit-realm that had a ripple effect, provoking a response from the heavenly and earthly realms.

Divine response

God then responds to Daniel's prayer by immediately sending the angel Gabriel to give Daniel an urgent and eschatological[67] message about the future of His people and the coming of the Messiah. (Daniel 9:24-27) But before the angel gives him this grand message, he first speaks something very personal to Daniel, from the Lord's heart: "Daniel, you are a man greatly beloved." (Daniel 9:23)

Oh, to hear those words from the mouth of the Lord! Before giving an assignment or a commission, God wanted to let Daniel know that all of heaven was moved by his life, declaring over him that he is highly esteemed, that he is beloved of the Lord. It is worth noting that the only two men in the Bible called "the Lord's beloved" are Daniel and the apostle John. (John 13:23, 20:2)

Both Daniel and John received detailed revelation concerning the end of the age, writing books in the Bible that contain key information about the Second Coming of Christ. Is there a connection between being near to the Lord's heart and being given access to the spirit of revelation that prepares us for the End Times?

John, in the book of Revelation, calls Satan "the accuser of the brethren." (Revelation 12:10) His accusations come not only against you and me, but sometimes even through you and me towards others. In 2 Timothy 3, Paul expounds on a warning that Jesus gave in Matthew 24, identifying the increasing "coldness" of heart that will mark the "last days" as being evidenced through unforgiveness, slander, gossip and betrayal. I believe that a personal revelation of God's Love, knowing our identity as the beloved of God, is essential in that it not only equips us to stand against the fiery darts of the enemy that we face daily, but actually guards us against the temptation to join with accuser against others. Intimacy with Jesus, a daily abiding in Christ, is our only guarantee for victory. [68]

Demonic response

James 5:16 says that the prayers of the righteous are powerful. Though unseen to most of us, demons respond to prayer, in opposition of course, creating war in heaven and strife on earth.[69] "Do you know why I [Gabriel] have come to you? Now I must return to fight with the prince of Persia ... Also, in the first year of Darius the Mede, I [Gabriel] even I stood up to confirm and strengthen him." (Daniel 11:1)

In heaven, as the angelic messenger was dispatched, the demonic principality, the prince of Persia, engaged in opposition, warring against the archangels Gabriel and Michael. What was the fight about? What was being stirred in the spirit realm? I would like to suggest that because of Daniel's prayer and the consequences of God's answer to that prayer, the kingdom of darkness was unleashed to resist and abort God's plan.

The demonic realm was fighting against Gabriel to prevent him from going to Daniel to deliver the message concerning the time of the end. (Dan 9:23-27) Was the enemy resisting the building of the temple? Yes, but more critically, there was a spiritual opposition to the return of Israel as a whole. Immediate resistance had to be enforced in an attempt to abort the seed, the coming Messiah, who would crush the serpent's head. (Genesis 3:15) The implications of Gabriel's message was essentially doom to the kingdom of darkness.[70]

The impact

The demonic realm has a natural influence on the earthly realm, using jealousy and pride as its main weapons.[71] The natural trigger in Daniel's situation (jealousy) was the fact that the king was promoting Daniel to the highest governmental position.(Daniel 6:3) Of course, this deeply upset the other high-ranking officials around the king, who would now have to subject themselves to a "Jewish captive." (Daniel 6:13) Jealousy opened the door of the soul to influence from the demonic realm. With violent thoughts controlling their emotions and minds, they devised an extreme two-step plan solely to get rid of Daniel: manipulate the king's power and incriminate Daniel.

First, they approached the king, dealing him the card of pride; they coddled his ego, hyping up the notion that he is not merely a man, but a god who alone is worthy of worship, alone to whom the people should "pray". The consequence for directing worship and prayer to another would be a visit to the lions' den. Darius loved the idea and signed a written decree. (Daniel 6:6-9)

Knowing Daniel's disciplined commitment to daily prayer, this was a guaranteed entrapment.

"Now when Daniel knew that the writing was signed, he went home. And in his upper room, with his windows open toward Jerusalem, he knelt down on his knees three times that day and prayed and gave thanks before his God, as was his custom since early days." (Daniel 6:10)

Fully knowing the content of the decree and its implications, he went on his knees "that day" with the windows open, unwilling to waver from the custom of his youth. What a powerful testimony of Daniel's character!

In their accusation of Daniel, they said, "Daniel, who is one of the exiles from Judah, pays no attention to you, O King." (Daniel 6:13) Hold on... Daniel had been a top leader in the government of three successive kings, within two empires. It had been decades since he was taken captive as a young man; why identify him with this label now? That is the way of the kingdom of darkness, firing accusations about the past, mixed with lies about Daniel's attitude and heart motivation.

Yet, according to the new law, Daniel was culpable. The king loved Daniel, so he was greatly displeased about the personal ramifications of his own decree, but he was forced to follow through with it. His own pride was now leading to the destruction of one of his most trusted and loyal advisers.

Daniel's spiritual conditioning

Unlike the Sunday school image, we all have in our minds of young Daniel in the lions' den, we need to remember that Daniel, at this point, is an old man in his eighties. The first year of Cyrus came seventy years after Daniel's captivity under the Babylonians.

This might seem like a random thought here, but here Daniel demonstrates an obscure spiritual principle that I want to highlight: one of the main spiritual battlefields in our lives is in the area of food.

Sin entered the world through a bite of a fruit. (Genesis 3:1-7) When Ezekiel listed the sins of Sodom, one would immediately think that it was sexual perversion. But that sin isn't even mentioned: "Look, this was the iniquity of your sister Sodom: She and her daughter had pride, fullness of food and abundance of idleness; neither did she strengthen the hand of the poor and needy ... they were haughty and committed abomination before Me." (Ezekiel 16:49,50) Does this resemble our western societies today?

The opposite of a "fullness of food" that opens the door to all kinds of gluttony is proven in Daniel's lifestyle of fasting. When you embrace the discipline to resist the temptation of food and intentionally abstain from certain pleasures (permissible and enjoyable), this can strengthen you to overcome other temptations. Because of his choice to abstain from the "delicacies of the king" when he was young, Daniel's soul was conditioned and strengthened to endure other hard choices and stand in the time of trouble. Now, as an elderly frail man, he was able to face this situation with loyalty to God, unmoved; even if it meant his body was going to be served as lunch for the lions.

A dear friend of mine, whom I greatly admire, has chosen to consecrate himself to the Lord in the area of fasting. For more than twenty years, he has chosen not to eat meat or drink red wine—two things that he really enjoys— not because he ever felt he was earning anything, but because he wanted to cultivate a deeper spiritual appetite. He has additionally done many extended water fasts. Like Daniel, he has chosen to let go of the "king's delicacies" for the purpose of "tasting" the sweetness of

God's word. Every time he speaks about the Word of God, in private or in public, there is an authority and a spirit of revelation that flows from his heart. His life of devotion and consecration challenges me; I want to be like him.

Years ago, as I was in the middle of an extended fast, I had a dream. In the dream, I was also fasting, but was very hungry. I was craving a big juicy cheeseburger but was trying to resist the temptation to eat it. I failed! I held it in my hands and took a large bite. Immediately, the scene changed and I was watching a Chinese believer who was in prison and the day of his martyrdom had come. I looked as I saw him stand by a wall in total surrender as the marksman was preparing his gun. I woke up immediately and the Lord spoke to me: "If you want to say YES to me and be ready to face the darkest moment of your life, you need to learn to say NO to that burger today."

I've learned that it is those small steps of disciplining our flesh today that prepares us to be steadfast and unwavering tomorrow. The battle is overcome in the belly before it's overcome in the den!

Divine decree

As they dropped Daniel to the hungry lions that eagerly waited for him and not knowing how many seconds he had to live, I could only assume that his prayer lingered in his heart. I don't think that it was a prayer for his life at that point. I think it was the prayer that he had already been willing to risk his life for: prayer for the salvation of Israel.

From the bottom of the pit, he continued as the lions refrained from attack, perhaps sitting in stillness next to him, listening to his appeal to God: "O Lord, hear! O Lord, forgive! O Lord, listen and act! Do not delay for Your own sake, my God, for Your city and Your people are called by Your name." (Daniel 9:19)

The king couldn't sleep and he spent the night fasting. Early the next morning, he went to the den and cried out, "Daniel, servant of the living God, has the God whom you serve continually been able to deliver you from the lions?" (Daniel 6:20) To his utter surprise, he heard Daniel's response: "My God sent his angel and shut the lions' mouths so that they have not hurt me because I was found innocent before Him and I have done no wrong before you." (Daniel 6:22)

The enemy tried to shut Daniel's mouth so he couldn't pray. Instead, God shut the lions' mouths so Daniel's prayer would prevail. Do you have a vision for your life to move heaven and earth? Do you have vision that your prayer life becomes a real threat to the kingdom of darkness and advances the purposes of God; that the effectiveness of your prayer life would leave the enemy terrified, even before you open your mouth to pray?

Darius's decree

Because of Daniel's faithfulness since the days of his youth, King Darius put his faith and trust in God bringing the Persian Empire under the authority and blessing of the Lord. Darius sent out a new decree: "...in every dominion of my kingdom, men must tremble and fear before the God of Daniel. For He is the living God and steadfast forever; His kingdom is the one which shall not be destroyed; His dominion shall endure to the end. He delivers and rescues and He works signs and wonders in heaven and on earth, who has delivered Daniel from the power of the lions." (Daniel 6:26,27)

Who heard this decree? The territory of the Persian Empire at the time included the present-day countries of Egypt, Iran, Israel, Saudi Arabia, Jordan, Iraq, Lebanon, Turkey, Armenia, Azerbaijan, Turkmenistan, Uzbekistan, Tajikistan, Afghanistan, Pakistan and parts of Kazakstan and India. Because of Daniel's prayers, the "10/40 Window"[72] of his day had a witness that Daniel's living God rescues, performs signs and wonders and has an everlasting dominion.[73]

Cyrus's decree

"Now in the first year of Cyrus king of Persia, that the word of the Lord by the mouth of Jeremiah might be fulfilled, the Lord stirred up the spirit of Cyrus king of Persia, so that he made a proclamation throughout all his kingdom... All the kingdoms of the earth the Lord God of heaven has given me. And He has commanded me to build Him a house at Jerusalem which is in Judah ... King Cyrus also brought out the articles of the house of the Lord, which Nebuchadnezzar had taken from Jerusalem..." (Ezra 1 :1-2, 7)

I cannot prove the sequence or timing of events, but I would like to propose that it would follow, that Isaiah's two-hundred-year-old prophetic word and Jeremiah's "seventy years" word were activated to come to pass when Daniel prayed (Daniel 9), in alignment with the timing of God. His prayer not only stopped the resistance of the kingdom of darkness, but also caused the hearts of kings to move. As Darius makes his decree from Babylon (Daniel 6), Cyrus is compelled to make a federal decree, not only permits Jews to return and rebuild, but he subsidizes the project with resources necessary to accomplish the work, including the confiscated sacred articles and treasures. (Ezra 1:7-11) The Persian rulers and the Persian people became a huge source of blessing in partnering with God's purposes for the Jewish people. (Daniel 6:28)

The people's response

"Then the heads of the fathers' houses of Judah and Benjamin and the priests and the Levites, with all whose spirits God had moved, arose to go up and build the house of the Lord which is in Jerusalem. And all those who were around them encouraged them with articles of silver and gold, with goods and livestock and with precious things, besides all that was willingly offered." (Ezra 1:5,6)

The human heart naturally responds to the wonders of God's movement and we see here that He was moving at every level. As the seventy-year captivity ended, the people were mobilised. Psalm 110 says; "People shall be volunteers in the day of Your power." The response of this generation is significant when you consider that their contributions to the rebuilding of the temple literally paved the way where Jesus would walk, centuries later, fulfilling prophecy. How are you responding to God's movement in your generation?

Our response

Daniel's prayer life was impactful, not only provoking the devil's assassination attempt, but this one man's steadfast obedience in prayer and fasting over decades brought forth a great breakthrough for generations to come.

Are we ready and aligned with heaven? How can we experience that same convergence between heaven and earth in our generation? We must give ourselves to the Word of God. God's word is true for all generations, but there is only one generation that will experience the fulfilment of the prophetic words related to the return of Christ. The Book of Daniel is so important to the End Time church, not only because of the information it contains, related to the second coming of the Lord, but also because of the lifestyle template it gives, preparing us as we expectantly wait for the return of the King.

Daniel prophesied that in the latter times, wisdom and understanding would increase as the books (held in heaven) are unsealed. (Daniel 12:9,10) As we approach that day, we must grow in our understanding of Scripture, praying God's word and prophetic promises until we see them manifest, whether in our lifetime or in a generation to come. We must grow in our identity as the beloved of God, live a holy, consecrated life and be fully given to prayer, fasting and feasting on the Word of God. Lord help!

I am confident that the global church will be equipped by the Holy Spirit to recognise times and seasons. We will grow in knowing what scriptures to pray and prophesy in each particular moment to bring His purposes to pass. At the fullness of time, the ultimate breakthrough will come, when the Bride, the Global Church, cries out in unison with the Holy Spirit, "Come, Lord Jesus, come!" (Rev 22:20) In that moment, He will split the sky and come down as the victorious and everlasting king!

ISRAEL, BORN IN EGYPT, RAISED IN IRAN

God is always after a deeper response from us, that of desperation and genuine worship.

Chapter 12

Iran: Where Worship Is Restored

God's Builders

"Many that hear this joyful sound, choose to sit still in Babylon, are in love with their sins and will not venture upon a holy life; but some break through all discouragements, whatever it cost them; they are those whose spirit God has raised above the world and the flesh, whom he has made willing. Thus, will the heavenly Canaan be filled, though many perish in Babylon; and the gospel offer will not have been made in vain."[74]
(Matthew Henry)

I love the power of imagination. What can become of what is before me? But imagination can also lead us to unrealistic expectations. Many of us have a certain idea of what our future should look like. When things don't go the way we expect at the pace we expect, or when sudden and surprising shifts happen, we can easily get confused, disoriented and become hopeless. On the other hand, it is possible to be caught up in the mundane, day-to-day events of life and find ourselves in a moment of breakthrough, fulfilment and/or answered prayer without recognising it, even when it is right before our eyes.

It is important to discern the moments we are living in, so we don't find ourselves living reactively but, rather, able to respond intentionally, even when our circumstances are not as we had hoped. On the other hand, a distorted understanding of what's happening around us can hinder us from taking an action that could propel us further into our destiny.

A reflection of the Jewish exile is a stark reminder of these truths. Following the Cyrus Declaration, the Jewish people throughout the empire now had the chance to return to their homeland. A dream come true? They had waited for this moment for seventy years. But sadly, most did not recognise the miracle at hand and lacked the vision and motivation to return.

Many scholars indicate that life for captives of the Babylonians was far from difficult. Many had freedom, economic opportunities and peace.[75] [76] Why would they leave the comfort of their adapted life in the most powerful empire on the planet? Why would they embark on a five-month journey, full of peril, to a desolate place? It required faith and character, to see what could become out of the rubble they were about to face. Only a small portion of the people said yes to this call and returned to build the temple and the city of Jerusalem.

Persian royal support

Cyrus, as mentioned in the previous chapter, was stirred by the Holy Spirit, in response to Daniel's prayer, to issue his decree for the rebuilding of the Jewish temple. He was not stirred momentarily by a whim of emotion; he had a resolve and a commitment to see this work finished. His decree, as we will see later, was crucial to guarantee the success of this work. It is one thing to have a conviction and another thing to follow that conviction with actions, especially actions that impact one's bank account.

"Let the expenses be paid from the king's treasury. Also let the gold and silver articles of the house of God, which Nebuchadnezzar took from the temple, which is in Jerusalem and brought to Babylon, be restored and taken back to the temple." (Ezra 6:3-5)

We can't underestimate the significance of this moment in natural and spiritual history. The Persians and their kings are forever recorded in the history books of heaven because of their participation with the work of grace and prompting of the Holy Spirit. This heathen king, Cyrus, is now God's "anointed" who responded to God's deep longing for His people to be set apart to host His presence. (Isaiah 45:1)

Israel's story was being "re-written". The captives were now free, not only to take back their land but to be restored as a nation of worship. For seventy years the people of God could not offer sacrifices, celebrate the feasts, nor corporately commune with God. But that was all changing. This was like the rebirth of the nation.

Who returned?

God was restoring the kingly and priestly bloodline within Israel. Leading the way back, he raised up Zerubbabel, a descendant of Jehoiachin, the king of Judah, (1 Chronicles 3:16-19) and Joshua, a descendant of Aaron, (Zechariah 3:1). Jeremiah had prophesied: "David will never fail to have a man to sit on the throne of Israel, nor will the Levitical priests ever fail to have a man to stand before me [the Lord] continually to offer burnt offerings, to burn grain offerings and to present sacrifices." (Jeremiah 33:17,18)

And so, the people returned, the work began and the altar was rebuilt. Morning and evening sacrifices resumed, the festivals kept and the people rejoiced. When the temple foundation was finally laid, there was a great celebration among the people, but the older priests and Levites who had seen the former temple wept aloud. (Ezra 3)

During a sovereign move of God, there will always be different dynamics, varied expectations, mixed emotions and frustrations. God never does the same thing twice. He is the Creator and His ways are always new. In contrast, we like to know what to expect, it helps us know how to respond. But God is always after a deeper response from us, that of desperation and genuine worship. He does things differently to test us and allow us to see what is hidden in the secret places of our soul.

There will also be opposition and a spiritual battle, sometimes for years, as in this case. During the reign of the king that followed Cyrus, the people of the land opposed this building project, so they wrote a letter to him, using the same strategy of lies and accusation that was used against Daniel (paraphrasing): "These people are rebuilding the rebellious city and its walls; if they are successful, they will not pay taxes to you. Because we care about you, we couldn't stand the idea of you being dishonoured that way, so we request that you immediately stop them." And so, the work stopped for the next sixteen years until the second year of Darius II of Persia.(Ezra 4)

God's heart displayed

During those long years, the people neglected the building project and instead focused on their own houses and personal livelihoods. After sixteen years, the Lord sent the prophets Haggai and Zechariah to call the people back to action.

"This people say, 'The time has not come ... that the Lord's house should be built' ... [but] Is it time for you yourselves to dwell in your panelled houses and this temple to lie in ruins? ... Consider your ways!" (Haggai 1:2-5)

You can hear the pain in the Lord's heart over the choices of His people. He was true to His word, fulfilling His promises to their father Abraham. But rather than advancing God's purposes, they gave in to outside pressures and retreated to focus on their own needs rather than on God's priorities.[77] These people had initially followed the call, paid a great price in leaving the comfort of Persia and started over with rubble. But in light of the current reality, they compromised. It's one thing to start well but another thing to end well. It's one thing to say yes to God's call but another thing to walk it out faithfully over decades.

The prophet Zechariah also came along with a message from God's heart, encouraging Zerubbabel to rise up and build: "'Not by might nor by power, but by My Spirit,' says the Lord of Hosts. 'Who are you, O great mountain [of rubble] before Zerubbabel? You shall become a plain! And he shall bring forth the capstone with shouts of "Grace, grace to it" ... The hands of Zerubbabel have laid the foundation of this temple; His hands shall also finish it... for who has despised the day of small things?'" (Zechariah 4: 6-10)

The people received the grace and the courage to respond again. Zerubbabel and Joshua, with all the remnant of the people, obeyed the voice of the Lord and rose up to build. Though their achievement may have seemed insignificant in comparison to the beauty of the former temple, the reality is that their work was directly paving the way for the coming of Messiah, the "Desire of All Nations" the fulfilment of all prophecy. The significance of the temple was not to be its size, but rather, the glory of the presence of God and the tangible result of His peace. (Haggai 2:3-9)

In our walk with God, we may never know where our small yes will lead us. God often works in our lives in small steps that, at times, may seem insignificant. The temptation is often to despise the smallness. But as we look back over the course of years, it becomes evident that He has been faithfully leading us. In the big picture plan of God to accomplish great things, He always chooses weak people, who need to do things one step at a time, looking at life circumstances through the eyes of faith, so they can keep building with Him, not giving up along the way. It will be faithful obedience that prepares us, as the Body of Christ, to welcome the King as He appears in ultimate triumph, with a glory that fills not just the temple but covers the whole earth as the waters cover the seas. (Habakkuk 2:14)

More opposition, greater breakthrough

As they rose up to build again, the accusations continued. King Darius conducted research, finding the original Cyrus decree confirming Cyrus's intent. Not only did Darius reinstate the old decree, but he also issued another, advancing Cyrus's legacy.

"For the building of this house of God: Let the cost be paid at the king's expense from taxes on the region beyond the river; this is to be given immediately to these men (the elders of the Jews) so that they are not hindered. And whatever they need—young bulls, rams, and lambs for the burnt offerings of the God of heaven, wheat, salt, wine and oil, according to the request of the priests who are in Jerusalem—let it be given them day by day without fail, that they may offer sacrifices of sweet aroma to the God of heaven and pray for the life of the king and his sons." (Ezra 6:8-12)

In an amazing turn of events, the king financed the continued building of the temple. Sixteen years before, the men of the region were accusing the Jews of not paying taxes; now their own taxes were financing the temple!

And thus, the building was complete, the priesthood was reinstated, the sacrifices were continually offered and, to top it all, the Passover feast was once again celebrated. God reminded them of his faithfulness, saying, "According to the word that I covenanted with you when you came out of Egypt, so my spirit, remains among you, do not fear." (Haggai 2:5)

He had faithfully led them out of Egypt and faithfully led them out of Persia. They had kept the new calendar that was divinely initiated as they left Egypt, when they celebrated the first Passover. Here, out of Persia, they celebrate it again and look ahead, by faith, to the appearance of the ultimate Passover lamb, when He would walk on the scene, down the halls of that very temple and declare that His house "shall be a house of prayer for all nations." (Isaiah 56:7; Matthew 21:13)

God remained committed to His people, raising up great men of character, Ezra and Nehemiah, who rose to the highest level in the Persian government during the reign of King Artaxerxes. They led the people back from exile, in the second and third waves of return, to rebuild the wall of the city as well as the spiritual life of the people despite the opposition from the surrounding peoples.[78]

The Persian Empire was divinely used by God to restore the temple, the priesthood, Jerusalem and the people. (Ezra 6:14-18) We should never undermine the significance of this for not only the Jewish people, but also for Iranians. I remember when the Lord called me to start praying for Iran, I started listening to Persian worship. I was undone. I have not experienced this in hearing other languages in worship. When they sing, there is a unique grace and anointing on the sound, the passion and the longing emanating from a place deep within the soul. I believe it has to do with the inheritance of the nation as it relates to worship, because of the significant investments over the years to revive the reality of worship for Israel. I believe the Lord has given believers in Iran a special anointing that is necessary to break through (whatever the barriers may be) and open hearts to a deeper intimacy with Jesus.

It is no wonder that Iran is governed by religious clergy. It affirms that the people of this nation have a destiny to be genuine worshippers. But I believe that her true identity will be restored as we continue to pray God's promises in Isaiah 19, declaring that there will be a worship highway from Egypt all the way to the farthest ends of the Assyrian region, encompassing Iran. I can't wait for the day when thousands of Egyptians, Iranians and Jews come together to worship Jesus, The King of Glory.

This one moment of favour with the king was a day on God's eternal calendar that was destined to shape history.

Chapter 13

Iran: Where Hearts Are Exposed

God's Queen

We all have calendars to manage our days, weeks and months and sometimes we can plan for certain events years ahead. But God knows the end from the beginning and He makes everything perfect in His time. (Isaiah 46:10; Ecclesiastes 3:11)

In His leadership over the nations, God looks for hearts that are willing to walk in faith and obedience, aligning their personal calendars with His. The story of Esther, Queen of Persia, is yet another vivid example of His sovereignty over time and space.

My first date with my wife-to-be was not necessarily on my calendar. Only an acquaintance at the time, I had emailed her and two other friends inviting them to join me at a local theatre to watch a movie that had just come out about the story of Queen Esther. At the last minute, the other two friends declined, which was to my advantage: now she and I were going on an "unplanned" first date. We had a great time together and that was the beginning of a beautiful courtship that has now blossomed into more than fifteen years of marriage. The story of our relationship is very special—but it will have to go in another book, as our focus here is on Esther's romance with the King of Persia.

Esther was a beautiful young Jewish orphan who was raised by her older cousin, Mordecai. Their families were exiled under the Babylonians and now were under the Persians during the reign of King Xerxes. At some point, the king divorced his queen, Vashti, because of her dissonant attitude, to say it nicely. Now, he was on a quest to find her replacement, sending his servants to scour the entire empire in search of the most beautiful young maidens. Only one would be chosen; the rest would be confined to the king's harem for the rest of their lives.

Esther, being one of the many candidates, was brought to the king's courts where she underwent a year-long beautification process in preparation to stand before him. Finally, the day came when both the earthly and the divine calendars aligned. Esther walked in before the king and God gave her favour in his eyes, opening his heart to choose her to be his wife and queen. This one moment of favour with the king was a day on God's eternal calendar that was destined to shape history.

The price of hatred

At the time of her reign, Esther's husband, King Xerxes, ruled over one hundred and twenty-seven nations. He had the largest empire the world has ever known, extending from India in the East all the way to Ethiopia in the South-west, with Susa as the capital (still a city in Iran today). One of his most trusted advisers was a powerful man by the name Haman,[79] who made his way up the political ladder, becoming second in command. Haman hated the Jews. This hatred was exacerbated by the fact that a Jew named Mordecai did not show him the honour he demanded. Enraged, Haman devised a plan to exterminate not only Mordecai, but all the Jews.

As we saw in a previous chapter, the Prince of Persia's resistance to Daniel manifested through the jealousy of the king's advisors. Once again, we see this played out through Haman's ego. He was under a demonic influence that was seeking to annihilate the Jewish people and prevent the coming of the promised seed. Taking advantage of his status, he approached the king, saying: "There is a certain people scattered and dispersed among the people in all the provinces of your kingdom; their laws are different from all other people and they do not keep the king's laws. Therefore, it is not fitting for the king to let them remain. If it pleases the king, let a decree be written that they be destroyed and I will pay ten thousand talents of silver into the hands of those who do the work, to bring it into the king's treasuries." (Esther 3:8-9)

Haman was willing to pay an equivalent of twenty-million dollars to kill the Jews! Oh, what a price for hatred! The king agreed to the plan, took the money and gave Haman his signet ring. And so, the death decree became a law that could not be altered or cancelled.

Upon hearing this terrible news, Mordecai mourned putting on sackcloth and ashes. He took the news to Esther, sensing perhaps she had been given a unique proximity to the king for such an important time as this. Mordecai challenged her to go before the king to persuade him to cancel the decree, insisting that God would save His people, but also warning that if she did not act, her life would not be spared. (Esther 4:14) Esther agreed, willing to take her chances. In preparation for her uninvited appearance before the king—an offence that could get her killed—she called a three-day fast among all the Jewish people in the Empire.

Open-ended questions

As this plot was festering, God was stirring the king's heart through a sleepless night. Restless, he asked for the book of remembrance to be read to him. In it was a record of a failed assassination; it was the loyalty of a certain man named Mordecai that saved his life. However, the record indicated that nothing had been done to honour this man's heroic actions. As the king pondered how to justify his debt to this man, Haman, perhaps sleepless himself, pays an early morning visit to suggest the hanging of a certain man named Mordecai. Before he could present his proposition, the king had a question for him: "What should be done for a man that the king delights to honour?" (Esther 6:6)

What kind of question was that? It was an open-ended question, the kind that stirs one's wildest imaginations. The answer could be anything, the king might grant whatever is spoken. It is like winning the lottery.

It reminds me of the night God spoke to Solomon saying, "Ask! What shall I give you?" Solomon responded saying, "You have shown great mercy to David my father and have made me king in his place ... now give me wisdom and knowledge, that I may go out and come in before this people." Then God replied, saying, "Because this was in your heart and you have not asked riches or wealth or honour or the life of your enemies, nor have you asked long life—but have asked wisdom and knowledge for yourself, that you may judge My people over whom I have made you king, wisdom and knowledge are granted to you; and I will give you riches and wealth and honour, such as none of the kings have had who were before you, nor shall any after you have the like." (2 Chronicles 1:7-12)

Unlike Solomon's humble response, Haman's heart was full of pride, thinking of only himself. Believing that there could be no better person whom the king would want to honour than him, he had a gaudy daydream about himself on the king's horse, wearing the king's garments, being honoured throughout the city. As he verbalised this, the king told him to immediately go and do just what he had spoken for a man named Mordecai. I can only imagine the look on Haman's face in that moment; I'll have to watch the movie again! It was a look of disgust, horror, unbelief and great rage, not only against Mordecai but against the king himself. With utter humiliation, his daydream turned into a real nightmare as he paraded his detested enemy around the city, crying out before him repeatedly, "THE KING DELIGHTS IN THIS MAN!"

The third day of Esther's fast had come. Esther made herself ready, put on her royal garments and made her way to the king's court uninvited. If the king does not extend the sceptre to her, she perishes. With one look into her eyes and a measure of divine favour to move his heart, the king lifts his hand to welcome her in. Then comes another open-ended question, this time to Esther: "What is your request? Ask up to half the kingdom and it will be given to you."

Revealing the heart

In that moment, Esther could have garnered land and wealth for herself and her people, perhaps much more than what was promised to Abraham. But what is the land without the people?

One main purpose for open-ended questions is to reveal a person's heart: what motivates their actions and desires? As we look at the answers Haman and Esther gave to these open-ended questions, we see a stark contrast. Their answers revealed the essence of their being.

Haman was only concerned with his ego and pride while Esther was willing to deny herself, even unto death. His pride led him to presumption and blindness: "Who else would the king honour more than me?" While her humility led her to complete surrender: "If I die, I die." He was concerned with self-exaltation while she was concerned with the wellbeing of others. He was motivated by jealousy and hatred, unto murder, while she was motivated by love and loyalty unto sacrifice.

What would your answer be if the Lord asked you an open-ended question today? Your answer to that question could determine not only your destiny, but that of many generations after you.

The truth is, God already knows what's in our hearts. Most of the time, however, we do not, or at least not fully. We need Him to ask those questions so that we can discover what He already knows about us, so that we can turn to Him and be healed. We need to have the courage that Esther had to surrender, lean into God, wait in His courts and be willing to honestly answer His open-ended questions. Like David, we need to regularly pray, "Search me, O God, and know my heart; Try me and know my anxieties, ... see if there is any wicked way in me, ... lead me in the way everlasting." (Psalm 139:23,24)

God's timely answer

Esther refused the appeal of half the kingdom. Her answer was a dinner invitation to the king and Haman. When they came to dinner, the king asked her once again what her true request was. She gave the same response. After the second dinner, in the presence of Haman, the king again offered her half of the kingdom. I wonder what Haman must have felt hearing this ongoing conversation and the impact of the blow that came when her true request was revealed:

"'If I have found favour in your sight, let my life be given to me at my petition, and my people at my request. For we have been sold, my people and I, to be destroyed, to be killed, and to be annihilated...' So, King Ahasuerus answered and said to Queen Esther, 'Who is he, and where is he, who would dare presume in his heart to do such a thing?' And Esther said, 'The adversary and enemy is this wicked Haman!'" (Esther 7:3-6)

Haman's nightmare turned to horror as the king realised that he had been manipulated to issue this decree. The king immediately ordered that Haman be hanged on the same pillar that was erected for Mordecai. Furthermore, he invited Mordecai to take Haman's position and all his possessions. Mordecai took the king's ring and signed another declaration stating that the Jews would be given the permission to defend themselves, in effect nullifying the death edict.

"So, Mordecai went out from the presence of the king in royal apparel of blue and white, with a great crown of gold and a garment of fine linen and purple... And in every province and city, wherever the king's command and decree came, the Jews had joy and gladness, a feast and a holiday. Then many of the people of the land became Jews, because fear of the Jews fell upon them." (Esther 8:15-17)

That day in the divine calendar was marked in earthly calendars from that day forward. The feast of Purim continues to be celebrated every year to this day.

Through Mordecai's stand to save the king's life, and Esther's stand to save her people, God had positioned a Jewish family to bring safety and stability to the royal family (and the Persian Empire). In turn, the Persian king would offer safety to all the Jewish people throughout the empire. Not only were the Jews saved, but through the witness of the Jewish people, the fear of God was put on display and many Persians from across the empire—putting their faith in Yahweh—looked forward for the promised Messiah to come. The blessing came full circle about four centuries later as Persian magi, seeing a sign of the fulfilment of this longing among the stars, travelled from Persia to Israel to honour the birth of the long-awaited King of kings!

A tension remains, however, in our day as we now wait for the return of the King. Would the enemy not again try to abort God's plan? When we look at the political landscape today between Iran and Israel, we must wonder if we are seeing the story of Esther, Mordecai and Haman playing out again in our generation. Years ago, the Shah of Iran, the last of a two thousand five hundred year-long Persian dynasty, was overthrown by the Islamic revolution, whose religious leaders govern Iran today. Their government has repeatedly taken a stance against Israel.

Throughout history, the enemy has repeatedly attempted to annihilate the Jews, or at least keep them out of Jerusalem, and, since the time of Christ, harden their hearts toward Yeshua. Perhaps the enemy has rationalised that if the conditions Jesus gave in Matthew 23:39 are not met, then Jesus cannot and will not come back.[80] Perhaps he will employ the Prince of Persia again to resist God's purposes.

Nevertheless, God is raising up a generation of Esthers and Mordecais. These are those who have, with purity of heart, passed the testing of open-ended questions, who have no personal agenda except the agenda of heaven, who will have the courage to stand in the day of trouble, not loving their lives even unto death. These ones will be aligned with the calendar of God, standing with the people of God, living for the purposes of God.

SHADI

Section 4
God's Inheritance
The New Testament and Beyond

"Remember the Law of Moses, My servant, which I commanded him in Horeb for all Israel, with the statutes and judgements. Behold, I will send you Elijah the prophet before the coming of the great and dreadful day of the Lord and he will turn the hearts of the fathers to the children and the hearts of the children to their fathers, lest I come and strike the earth with a curse."(Malachi 4:4-6)

These were the very last words recorded in the Old Testament under the Persian Empire. In them, the prophet Malachi was tying together the bookends of the Old Testament and the journey of Israel. He was connecting the past to the present, linking Israel's coming out of Egypt to serve the Lord, with a call to the future generations to return to Him and look ahead toward the fulfilment of the promise.

Almost four hundred years of divine prophetic silence followed. That silence was similar, in some ways, to the four hundred years of silence that Israel endured as slaves in Egypt before the deliverer arose. In the meantime, the Persians lost their world dominance to the Greeks; they, in turn, lost it to the Romans, exactly as prophesied by Daniel,[81] marking an end of an era awaiting the coming of Messiah, "The Hope of Israel." (Jeremiah 14:8, 17:13)

Divine order speaks, even through chasms of silence.

Chapter 14

Between Egypt and Iran: The Advent of Messiah

Around the same time that Queen Esther was ruling in Persia, under the security and protection offered by the Persian Empire, Malachi, the last prophet in the Old Testament, arose in Jerusalem prophesying:

"I will send my messenger and he will prepare the way before me and the Lord who you seek will suddenly come to His temple. Even the messenger of the covenant in whom you delight. Behold He is coming, says the Lord of hosts, but who can endure the day of his coming." (Malachi 3:1)

The connected destiny between Egypt and Iran did not end with the Old Testament. Even in the fulfilment of God's plan for Israel to bring forth the Messiah, Egypt and Iran continue to be intimately involved in the events of the birth and the preservation of the Christ-child.

Mark starts his gospel by quoting the prophets Malachi and Isaiah, declaring the arrival of John as the embodiment of the voice coming out of the wilderness, crying, "Prepare ye the way of the Lord!" [82] Luke picks up the same quote from Malachi and identifies who broke that four-century-long silence: it was the voice of the angel Gabriel. (Luke 1:1-23)

Gabriel's last appearance in biblical text was centuries earlier, when he stood before Daniel in Persia. Now he was sent to visit an elderly man by the name Zechariah, declaring: "I am Gabriel, who stands in the presence of God...sent to speak to you and bring you these glad tidings." (Luke 1:19)

Breaking the silence

Zechariah was a priest and his wife, Elizabeth, was a daughter of Aaron, both from the tribe of Levi. They were blameless before the Lord but had no children. "As he was serving the Lord according to the division of Abijah, according to the custom of the priesthood, his lot fell to burn incense when he went into the temple of God." (Luke 1:5)

1 Chronicles 24 lists the order of worship established by David, according to which the priesthood would minister in the tabernacle and later in the temple. Each priestly family was assigned a specific time in the year to minister to the Lord. The division of Abijah was the eighth in the order. (1 Chronicles 24:10) That order was probably restored after the exiles returned. We know that not all returned to the ruins of Jerusalem, so it is fascinating to see that among the remnant, the priestly lineage of Abijah, was stirred to return. (Nehemiah 12:4,17)

Divine order speaks, even through chasms of silence. He had preserved the lineage of Aaron in Egypt and again in Iran so that in the fullness of time, through the priestly order of Abijah (which literally means "God is my father"), Zechariah would stand, chosen by a drawing of lots, to minister in the temple of the Lord. Gabriel broke the silence of heaven, giving Zechariah an epic message of a promised miracle-son:

"...You will have joy and gladness and many will rejoice at his birth. For he will be great in the sight of the Lord... he will also be filled with the Holy Spirit, even from his mother's womb and he will turn many of the children of Israel to the Lord their God. He will also go before Him in the spirit and power of Elijah, 'to turn the hearts of the fathers to the children,' and the disobedient to the wisdom of the just, to make ready a people prepared for the Lord." (Luke 1:13-17)

Yet, Zechariah, overwhelmed and struggling to believe the messenger, came out of the temple silent for the next nine months. Perhaps Zechariah's silence was more than a discipline or reprimand of the Lord, but a prophetic hush on earth, preparing for the voice that would soon cry out.

That earthly hush was broken at John's birth, as Zechariah's tongue was loosed to utter these prophetic words:

"Blessed is the Lord God of Israel, for He has visited and redeemed His people, ... to remember His holy covenant, the oath which He swore to our father Abraham: to grant us, that we, being delivered from the hand of our enemies, might serve Him without fear, in holiness and righteousness ... and you, child, will be called the prophet of the Highest; for you will go before the face of the Lord to prepare His ways, to give knowledge of salvation to His people by the remission of their sins..." (Luke 1:68-79)

The Birth of the King

Dispatched as the carrier of all Messiah-related news, Gabriel's next stop was Nazareth, to a young girl named Mary.

"...Behold, you will conceive in your womb and bring forth a Son and shall call His name Jesus. He will be great and will be called the Son of the Highest; and the Lord God will give Him the throne of His father David. And He will reign over the house of Jacob forever and of His kingdom there will be no end." (Luke 1:31-33)

There is no indication of a heavenly battle around the delivery of Gabriel's message, as in the days of Daniel, but there was a sign in the heavens detected by a group of Persian Magi. It is not clear whether these men were of a historic or ethnically Persian background, or if they were Jewish descendants of exiles who remained in Persia post-exile. Regardless, I believe God was intentionally weaving the Persians into this part of the storyline because of their history of honouring, blessing and preserving His people.

An extraordinary "star" was heralding the fulfilment of centuries of prophecy in the night sky over Persia. These men were among the first to recognise the announcement of the birth of the Isaiah 9:6 Messiah, even before the priests and scribes in Israel.

As they got the memo about the baby shower of the ages, they loaded their camels with gifts that showed that they understood who Jesus was called to be: gold for the King of kings, frankincense for the Great High Priest and Myrrh for the Lamb of God.[83] Perhaps the greatest gift they offered was deciding not to return to Herod after they had found the infant King. Sensing there was evil in his heart, and being instructed by an angel, they returned directly to Persia. Their silence in that moment, preserved and rescued Jesus and his family from annihilation. Herod, in turn, sent the sword throughout the region, killing every male child in Bethlehem under two years of age. Once again, we see Persians positioned to preserve the seed of Abraham.

An angel also appeared to Joseph, instructing him to go to Egypt with Jesus and Mary. (Matthew 2:13-15) Egypt had partnered with God's purposes for His people over the years; now God would send His only begotten Son into their land to grow up there, drink from the Nile, perhaps learn the Egyptian language and deposit a portion of His hidden glory and holy presence in this nation.[84]

How did Jesus and his family survive in Egypt? How were they financed as refugees? It was likely the Persian gold received from the Magi that sustained them. Eventually, they made their way back to Israel, fulfilling Hosea's words, "Out of Egypt I have called my Son." (Hosea 11:1; Matthew 2:15) And, thus, we see that in the life of Christ himself, God positioned both Iran and Egypt to once again be a safe highway and a source of provision, preparing the way of the Lord.[85]

The Baptism of water and fire

The Baptism of Jesus by John was more than a religious act. It was an alignment of heaven and earth as Jesus the Son submitted to the will of the Father as His voice thundered from heaven, reverberating on earth from eternity: "This is my beloved Son in whom I am well pleased." (Matthew 3:17) His voice would never again be silent. In the past, He had spoken through His holy prophets, but now He was speaking through His Son, the Word, breaking the deafening silence once and for all! (Hebrews 1:1-2; John 1:1)

John had declared, "He who comes after me, will baptise you with Holy Spirit and Fire." (Matthew 3:11) After His crucifixion, before Jesus departed to heaven, His Jewish disciples were all commissioned to go into all the nations. As they waited for the "Promise of the Father" there suddenly came "a sound from heaven of a rushing mighty wind ... then there appeared to them divided tongues, as of fire ... and they were all filled with the Holy Spirit and began to speak with other tongues, as the Spirit gave them utterance." (Acts 2:1-4)

Yet again, silence was broken; this time to announce the Good News to all the nations by the mouth of the apostles speaking in foreign languages. Parthians, Elamites and Medes (three people groups in Iran) were the first nations listed with the Egyptians, among other people groups that were present that day. Thus, the church in Iran, Egypt [86] and in the nations was birthed as three thousand people put their faith in the risen Jewish Messiah.

ISRAEL, BORN IN EGYPT, RAISED IN IRAN

Just as we have seen "Ishmael" carry Joseph into his inheritance and fullness, once again, God will use the "Ishmaelite" nations around Israel to bring her into fullness.

Chapter 15

Between Egypt and Iran: The Reign of Messiah

"I am the root and the offspring of David."
(Rev 22:16)

These are Jesus's last words in the book of Revelation. As He gives details of His return, Jesus reminds us of His divine origin and His human lineage. He is the one that created David and at the same time, He is also the son of David. The mystery of the incarnation will always blow our minds away as we seek to comprehend the magnitude and implications of what really happened when the Son of God willingly chose to put on flesh. Jesus will be fully God and fully man forever. At the nucleus of His humanity is Jewish DNA. The I Am, the Angel of the Lord, the Ancient of days, was manifest in the flesh and in Him all the fullness of God was manifest. (Colossians 1:15-19)

Jesus's own words about Himself echo what Isaiah had prophesied about Him centuries before: "For unto us a Child is born, unto us a Son is given; and the government will be upon His shoulder. His name will be called Wonderful, Counsellor, Mighty God, Everlasting Father, Prince of Peace. Of the increase of His government and peace there will be no end; upon the throne of David and over His kingdom, to order it and establish it with judgement and justice from that time forward, even forever." (Isaiah 9:6,7)

As mentioned throughout this book, the main purpose of God's choosing the people of Israel was to bring forth the Messiah, the King and the Saviour of the world. Most of the Jewish people of His day did not recognise Him when He came in humility. They were expecting a king to conquer their political enemies and sit on the throne of David but, instead, he was led as a lamb to the slaughter. (Isaiah 53) What they missed was the fact that the Messiah would come twice. The first time in humiliation, the second time in glory, coming back to Jerusalem, defeating all evil, destroying death and establishing His Kingdom on earth as it is in heaven.

Before His crucifixion, Jesus declared to the people of Jerusalem, "You shall not see Me again until you say, 'Blessed is He who comes in the name of the Lord!'" (Matthew 23:39) Here He is quoting a prophetic psalm of David, Psalm 118, which He had referenced a few days earlier when He entered Jerusalem confronting the religious leaders. (Matthew 21)

There, Jesus referred to himself as the chief cornerstone, the foundation of all things; though "the builders rejected" it, the Lord would reveal something "marvellous". The Psalmist declares that the people would bless this one "who comes in the name of the Lord" from the "house of the Lord". In essence, using the language of the Psalmist, Jesus is saying three things: He is coming back; returning to Jerusalem; and Jewish people in Jerusalem will recognise Him as their Messiah. These three things are all prerequisites for His return.

Peter underscores Jesus's words, connecting the return of the Messiah to Israel's recognition of Jesus as the appointed deliverer.

"Now, fellow Israelites, I know that you acted in ignorance, as did your leaders, but this is how God fulfilled what he had foretold through all the prophets, saying that his Messiah would suffer. Repent, then and turn to God, so that your sins may be wiped out, that times of refreshing may come from the Lord and that he may send the Messiah, who has been appointed for you— even Jesus. Heaven must receive him until the time comes for God to restore everything, as he promised long ago through his holy prophets." (Acts 3:17-21, NIV)

Zechariah, being one of these prophets whom Peter mentions, declares that there will be a supernatural grace released on the "house of David" and all of Jerusalem for a mournful turning and crying out when they see their Messiah: "Then they will look on Me, the one whom they pierced. Yes, they will mourn for Him as one mourns for his only son and grieve for Him as one grieves for a firstborn." (Zechariah 12:10) To date, this has not occurred. We see that Scripture clearly connects this "turning" of Israel to the future return of Christ.

How will they hear?

The testimony of the surrounding nations, especially those in closest proximity to Israel, will be one of the primary catalysts quickening the revelation that Jesus is, in fact, her Messiah. And so, it stands to reason that the

Middle East will take centre stage during the events leading up to Christ's second coming.

"I say then, have they stumbled that they should fall? Certainly not! But through their fall, to provoke them to jealousy, salvation has come to the Gentiles. Now, if their fall is riches for the world and their failure riches for the Gentiles, how much more their fullness... blindness in part has happened to Israel until the fullness of the Gentiles has come in. And so, all Israel will be saved ... For as you Gentiles were once disobedient to God, yet have now obtained mercy through their disobedience, even so these also have now been disobedient, that through the mercy shown you they also may obtain mercy." (Romans 11:11,12, 25-31)

This provocation would not be primarily an intellectual persuasion but rather a rousing of desire caused by the power of love demonstrated through lives laid down to serve the Jewish people. A generation of "Ruths" will rise up saying, "Your God is my God and your people are my people." (Ruth 1:16) As we lay down our lives for their sake, the love of God will pierce their hearts and their eyes will be opened.[87] Just as we have seen "Ishmael" carry Joseph into his inheritance and fullness, once again, God will use the "Ishmaelite" nations around Israel to bring her into fullness.

Context for provocation

Regardless of your personal views, as I delve into the realm of eschatology, it is my conviction that Scripture is clear about a progression of events leading to the "end of the story". Having a conviction that these events have happened, will happen or are a spiritual, not a physical, reality does not permit us to dismiss these scriptures, or the themes highlighted through them. We want to embrace and reach to understand the fullness of God's heart through the fullness of His Word.[88]

The Bible clearly teaches that, preceding the coming of the Lord, there will be a context of intense circumstances known as the "great tribulation". As we approach this period of history, I believe that God will prepare the nations in a unique way for the "Great and Terrible" Day of the Lord.[89]

In Matthew 21, Jesus prophesies that the difficulties that Israel and the nations will face will surpass those of any other time in history, with massive numbers of martyrs. The main source of antagonism and anguish will be the rise of the Antichrist and his global empire. If you recall, the Angel Gabriel appeared to Daniel giving him a message with precise details of some of those events.

"He shall speak pompous words against the Most High, shall persecute the saints of the Most High ... the saints shall be given into his hand..." (Daniel 7:25)

"Then he shall confirm a covenant with many for one week; But in the middle of the week. He shall bring an end to sacrifice and offering." (Daniel 9:27)

Paul similarly exhorts the church to be watchful and alert, understanding that Christ will return to bring justice and establish righteousness only after the rise of the 'son of perdition'. That term is believed by many scholars to be a reference to the Antichrist.

"Let no one deceive you by any means; for that Day [the coming of the Lord] will not come unless the falling away comes first and the man of sin is revealed, the son of perdition, who opposes and exalts himself above all that is called God or that is worshipped, so that he sits as God in the temple of God, showing himself that he is god... and then the lawless one will be revealed, whom the Lord will consume with the breath of His mouth and destroy with the brightness of His coming." (2 Thessalonians 2:3,4,8)

The epicentre of these events will be Jerusalem, where Jesus is coming back to establish His Millennial reign from the City of the Great King. (Psalm 48:2, Matthew 5:35)

For centuries, there has been contention over this city, yet the days ahead will witness unprecedented spiritual and physical battles. (Zechariah 14) It would follow, then, that the Jewish people will face dire and extreme circumstances, (perhaps more than anywhere else in the world) leading some to flee their homes seeking refuge in the surrounding lands for a season.

"For I will gather all the nations to battle against Jerusalem; the city shall be taken, the houses rifled and the women ravished. Half of the city shall go into captivity, but the remnant of the people shall not be cut off from the city." (Zechariah 14:2)

After these events and in this context, the Bible refers to a large-scale Jewish exodus from Israel's neighbouring countries. Whatever one's interpretation of these verses, whether it was partially or fully realised with the Jewish people's return to the land after 1948, I believe it is in keeping with God's heart that he would position these nations to shelter and comfort Israel in future distress. (Isaiah 40:1, 27-31) It is no surprise that we find Egypt and Iran listed among the empathetic nations.

"The Lord shall set his hand again the second time to recover the remnant of his people who are left from Assyria and Egypt, from Pathros and Cush, from Elam [Iran] ... there will be a highway for the remnant of his people who will be left from Assyria as it was for Israel in the day that he came up from the land of Egypt." (Isaiah 11:11-16)

"But it shall come to pass in the latter days, I will bring back the captives of Elam [Iran] says the Lord." (Jeremiah 49:39)

"As in the days when you came out of the land of Egypt, I will show them wonders." (Micah 7:15)

"I will strengthen the house of Judah, And I will save the house of Joseph. I will bring them back, because I have mercy on them ... I will sow them among the peoples And they shall remember Me in far countries; They shall live, together with their children And they shall return. I will also bring them back from the land of Egypt And gather them from Assyria." (Zechariah 10:6-10)

"So it shall be in that day: The great trumpet will be blown; They will come, who are about to perish in the land of Assyria and they who are outcasts in the land of Egypt and shall worship the Lord in the holy mount at Jerusalem." (Isaiah 27:13)

While we clearly see that prior to the return of Christ, Egypt and Iran will be used of God once again to be a source of provision and sustenance for the Jewish people, we know the current reality of hostilities, mistrust and woundedness that exists in the region. We must consider what needs to occur within the Church of these nations to awaken them and prepare their hearts to welcome their Jewish family, despite the danger and the cost. The Church is beckoned to not be surprised by these events, but to be prepared. This is not so much a preparation for physical survival, but for a strength of spirit and soul to endure, as Daniel, Esther and those who have gone before.

We must pray for the church in the Middle East to receive revelation, courage and a compelling love. We have confidence in the Lord's faithfulness to complete what He started as Isaiah 19 sheds light on the glorious reality ahead of the Church. At the centre of the Lord's plans being carried out among the nations, Israel, Egypt and Assyria will demonstrate the greatest international, spiritual and social miracle in history, as the Lord cultivates a profound unity and spiritual maturity among them.[90] Even at the end of the age, God has positioned Egypt and Iran to be a blessing, not only for but together with Israel.

The return of the King

"Immediately after the tribulation of those days ... the sign of the Son of Man will appear in heaven and then all the tribes of the earth will mourn and they will see the Son of Man coming on the clouds of heaven with power and great glory." (Matthew 24:29,30)

These are Jesus's own words, prophesying about himself with a quote from the book of Daniel.

"Behold, One like the Son of Man, Coming with the clouds of heaven. He came to the Ancient of Days And they brought Him near before Him. Then to Him was given dominion and glory and a kingdom, that all peoples, nations and languages should serve Him. His dominion is an everlasting dominion, which shall not pass away, And His kingdom the one Which shall not be destroyed." (Daniel 7:13,14)

At the sound of the last trumpet, Jesus will appear in the sky, descend to earth, resurrect the saints, defeat all His enemies and establish His eternal reign. The family of Abraham will once and for all be united, as the Kingdom of God is being fully revealed, satisfying the Father's heart.

We started this chapter with the last words of Jesus in the book of Revelation; it is fitting to end with His first words:

"From Jesus Christ, the faithful witness, the firstborn from the dead and the ruler over the kings of the earth. To Him who loved us and washed us from our sins in His own blood and has made us kings and priests to His God and Father, to Him be glory and dominion forever and ever.

Amen. Behold, He is coming with clouds and every eye will see Him, even they who pierced Him. And all the tribes of the earth will mourn because of Him. Even so, Amen. 'I am the Alpha and the Omega, the Beginning and the End,' says the Lord, 'who is and who was and who is to come, the Almighty.'" (Revelation 1:5-8)

ISRAEL, BORN IN EGYPT, RAISED IN IRAN

The journey of His People, Israel, between Egypt and Iran finds its fullness in Him.

Conclusion

Tying It All Together

I pray that this book has been a blessing to you and that my own journey can serve to propel you a little further in your walk with God, particularly in understanding His purposes for your own life as it relates to His purposes for the Middle East.

"Therefore, remember that you, once Gentiles in the flesh —who are called Uncircumcision by what is called the Circumcision made in the flesh by hands— that at that time you were without Christ, being aliens from the commonwealth of Israel and strangers from the covenants of promise, having no hope and without God in the world. But now in Christ Jesus you who once were far off have been brought near by the blood of Christ. For He Himself is our peace, who has made both one and has broken down the middle wall of separation, having abolished in His flesh the enmity, that is, the law of commandments contained in ordinances, so as to create in Himself one new man from the two, thus making peace and that He might reconcile them both to God in one body through the cross, thereby putting to death the enmity. And He came and preached peace to you who were far off and to those who were near. For through Him we both have access by one Spirit to the Father. Now, therefore, you are no longer strangers and foreigners, but fellow citizens with the saints and members of the household of God, having being built on the foundation of the apostles and prophets, Jesus Christ Himself being the chief cornerstone, in whom the whole building, being fitted together, grows into a holy temple in the Lord, in whom you also are being built together for a dwelling place of God in the Spirit!" (Ephesians 2:11-22)

This passage of scripture sums up many themes highlighted throughout the book. As we conclude, I want to leave you with a few takeaway points.

Abraham's children

We started this journey by looking at Abraham's children and how God sovereignly connected them for the purpose of establishing Israel as a nation of worship. Ishmael, Isaac and Midian were very key in their role of preserving the promised seed and establishing the nation of Israel at her infancy. Their submission and co-operation with the grace and plan of God brought forth a breakthrough for the nation of Israel and ultimately the Messiah's first coming. That relationship does not stop there. Even at the end of the age, God will bring all of Abraham's children together. As Jews will be provoked to eagerly receive their Messiah and enter into worship with their brothers—as described in Isaiah 19—the sons of Abraham, through their profound coming together, will release a blessing to the whole earth. The fullness of this will be directly connected to Messiah's second coming.

God's sovereignty over the nations

It is difficult to imagine what Israel would be without Egypt and Iran. These nations are so integral to her story. Additionally, without Israel, there would be no hope that has come to the nations through her Messiah. Regardless of what nation or people you are born into, God is in charge. The earth and its fullness belong to Him. He keeps installing rulers and deposing them. He is guiding history to His ultimate goal. We shouldn't have any doubts that Jesus remains seated upon His throne, unmoved and undisturbed, even in the face of unjust and corrupt world governments. He is the King of all kings. Because He controls the intended outcome, He looks down and laughs at the varied plots because He knows that He has been promised the ownership of the entire planet. (Psalm 2) So, we can confidently join Him in prayer, saying, "Your kingdom come, your will be done on earth as it is in heaven." (Matthew 6:10)

Anointed sons and daughters

The Lord raised Ezra and Nehemiah to serve in high governmental positions. He appointed Joseph and Esther to bring deliverance. He set Daniel and his friends in positions of favour with their king. These stories we read are not just nice fairytales, the kind where the underdog—the orphan, the dreamer—is finally realised and rises to the top. We see in them an everlasting God story, intricately weaving together great details to demonstrate God's sovereignty and desire for every nation. The Lord accomplishes His purposes throughout all time through His people, but I believe that, according to Joel 2:28-29,

Daniel 11:33 and 12:9-10, the End Time church will stand, having being tested and tried, walking in a greater measure of fullness, having learned to remain in Christ and daily gain their sustenance from Him. God will again exalt Josephs, Daniels and Esthers, set them before rulers and cause them to deliver kingdom solutions in the middle of worldwide catastrophe.

An Esther moment

Esther's life in Persia was a prophetic message to the generation in the last days. Like Esther, the global bride is being prepared, refined and purified.[91] Her willingness to die for the cause reflects the saints' "not loving their life even unto death." (Revelation 12:10) The intensifying of prayer and fasting in her life is reflected in Jesus' command to "watch and pray".[92] The breakthrough comes as God destroys the enemy in one day, transfers the power to His people as He hosts a great banquet filled with joy and gladness.[93] I believe that we are approaching an Esther moment in history, when we will have to declare our allegiance to the Lord and take a stand for Him: what and who He stands for. Hence, we must overcome our personal barriers to be able to agree with His heart, His purposes and His timing, to be able to respond rightly in the critical moments. I also believe that the women of Iran will have a major role in this. They will raise up their voices to sing the song of the Lord, even in the watches of the night, joining the daughters of Jerusalem in their song.[94] Together, having their lamps filled with the prepared oil of Matthew 25, they will receive the bridegroom when He comes and all the nations will sing, welcoming our Jewish king to Jerusalem: "Hosanna, blessed is He who comes in the name of the Lord!" (Matthew 21:9)

Jesus, the All in All

Jesus Christ (born in Bethlehem, given refuge in Egypt, raised in Nazareth) is the seed that was promised to Abraham. He is the fulfilment of the Law and the Prophets. He is the incarnate Son of God, He is the coming king, He is the firstborn of many brothers (Romans 8:29) and the firstborn of the dead (Colossians 1:18); He is the all in all. Jesus Christ is the culmination of all things. The Historical Jewish Yeshua of Nazareth; the Abiding Yeshua, who dwells within us by the Holy Spirit; and the Eschatological Yeshua, who is returning in power and glory, is the same yesterday, today and forever. From His first appearance to Hagar as the Angel of the Lord, to His incarnation, to the outpouring of His Holy Spirit, to His glorious return, He repeatedly honours Egypt and Iran, choosing them to serve, not only His purposes for the nation of Israel, but to serve Him personally. The journey of His People, Israel, between Egypt and Iran finds its fullness in Him.

Notes

Preface

[1] It must be noted that the Middle East is home to many tribes and ethnicities. Generally, people clump all of the ethnic groups together and call them Arabs, perhaps because what connects them now is the Arabic language, but that is not really an accurate one-size-fits-all label. However, for simplicity, I may still use the term 'Arabs' or 'Ishmaelites' when referring "broadly" to the nations/historic ethnicities surrounding Israel.

[2] As a point of preface, Isaiah 19 refers to the geographical boundary-lines of the Assyrian empire at the time it was written. For the purposes of this book, I have chosen to highlight the specific area of what was the far-eastern geographical area of "Assyria," now within the borders of modern-day Iran. By this, I am not limiting God's purposes to a broad or narrow definition of "Assyria" as referenced in Isaiah 19 (this could span a large area of what today reaches Jordan/Saudi up to Turkey/Azerbaijan). I also highlight Iran because of the specific ethnic, cultural, and historical link as descendants of the Persian/Achaemenian Family.

[3] Jesus would later reveal that He is the living water and all who drink of the water He gives would never thirst again, and, indeed, they themselves would have within them an everlasting fountain. (John 4:14)

Chapter 1

4 Recent policy changes in the region, initiated by a few Arab nations, have opened up new doors for travel and business, i.e. Abraham Accords. This unimaginable step forward will hopefully create more opportunity for understanding and appreciation.

5 Esau lost his birthright to Jacob. Esau's descendants (Edomites, from Edom) are the fathers of Arab tribes in Jordan today. During the time of the Exodus, Edom refused to assist the Israelites in their journey, and remained antagonistic toward Israel throughout history.

6 Though this wound is very difficult to heal, I have seen Jews and Arabs come together in love, humility and complete surrender to the redeeming work of the Cross of Christ—the only hope for true and lasting healing.

7 I believe that the weight of Scripture, especially in light of the many unfulfilled prophetic promises related to the second coming of Christ, is clear in asserting that Israel has a distinctive role in the fulfillment of Scripture. Paul also makes it clear that as the global church is grafted into our Jewish roots, we will walk into the fulness of our inheritance only together as one new man, Jew and Gentile, manifesting the Kingdom of God. See Ephesians 2 and Romans 11.

8 Though I had done my research and there were many nearly-miraculous confirmations, making it evident that this was God's leading, because of my offense, I began questioning God and His heart for me. That is the way offense works.

[9] Messianic Jews define themselves as ethnic jews who have put their faith in Jesus Christ (Yeshua) as the Messiah spoken of in the Law and Prophets.

Chapter 2

[10] See Ephesians 4:11-16.

[11] See Ezra 6:3-5; Ezra 1:1-11; Isaiah 44:28-45:1-4.

[12] I believe we will see this economic highway between these three nations reemerge once again as we approach the return of the Lord.

[13] Starting with His response to the cries of Israel in Egypt, we see that God uses this endearing term for Israel particularly when speaking to her in seasons of torment (i.e. by the Philistines in 1 and 2 Samuel), correction (1 and 2 Chronicles) and when the Lord issues a decree of comfort in Isaiah 40:1.

[14] Throughout the Middle East today, a prayer and worship movement is arising, especially among young people, who understand this passage and the significance of its fulfillment. God will bring His children together above the historic and religious conflicts, to release a blessing in the midst of the earth.

Chapter 3

[15] See Genesis 25:12-18, 1 Chronicles 1:28-31.

[16] Esau inhabited Seir, located in modern day Jordan. Genesis 33:16.

[17] See Genesis 25:2-4,18 and 1 Chronicles 1:32,33.

Chapter 4

[18]See Genesis 17:5

Abram means "exalted father."

Abraham means "chief of multitudes."

[19]See Genesis 15.

[20]Adding the *H* in the name invokes the name "Yahweh," identifying that person as belonging to God.

Chapter 5

[21]*Ishmael* means "the God who hears."

[22]This statement is made in the Surah Ikhlas (Arabic text: (الْإِخْلَاص), the 112th Surah of the Qur'an.

[23]The Muslim people refer to themselves as the sons of Ishmael.

[24]I encourage you to invest time in learning about the people, the culture, the needs of specific countries or people groups - there is quite a spectrum and we have found that informing our prayer helps to sustain our hearts. There are many resources such as Prayercast.com, 30 Days of Prayer for the Muslim World (pray30days.org), among many others.

Chapter 6

[25]See Chapter 3 in this book for a recap on this theme.

[26]See Romans 11:11,12.

27*Kairos* (Ancient Greek: καιρός) means "the right, critical, or opportune moment."

Chapter 7

28While it is commonly known that the Egyptian mummification process took 70 days, the text points out that Jospeh requested that his physicians attend the body, not the Egyptian priests - perhaps the process was not the complete or traditional mummification process.

Chapter 8

29I wonder if this ancient Egyptian law laid the foundation for our laws today regarding abortion, some of which even allow killing babies after they are born. Even as these types of decrees are trending again in our modern society, we see there is again a need for a deliverance.

30Genesis 37:25-28.

31See Ezekiel 28:13-15.

32YAHWEH or JEHOVAH Means "the Eternal One, the Unchangeable One, the One Who was, and is, and is to come; The One from everlasting to everlasting, the I Am that I am."

33See Cooper.

34Joel Richardson, among others, has done quite a bit of research and exploration on the ground. You can research his findings to learn more. Richardson, Joel. *Mount Sinai in Arabia: The True Location Revealed.* Winepress, 2019.

---

[35]See Chapter 5.

[36]The "Pharaohs" symbolise the systems of bondage and slavery that are ever increasing in our world.

Chapter 9

[37]Arnold 590.

[38]From here, we will refer to the southern kingdom of Judah as Israel.

[39]See commentary on Zedekiah.

[40]See Bradshaw.

[41]"Nebuchadnezzar is referred to as "My servant" in Jeremiah 25:9.

[42] Herodotus 239-241.

[43]See Gurney.

[44]See Henry (*Commentary*).

[45]See Storms.

[46]Anderson 123-129.

[47]Olmstead 50.

[48]See "Cambyses."

[49]Olmstead 107.

[50]See Coffman

[51]See Nehemiah 1-13 and Ezra 7- 10.

[52]Huntzinger 53-55.

[53] Sources for Timeline data: Constable (*Notes on Ezra* and *Notes on Daniel*) and House and Mitchell 174.

[54]There are many educational resources available for further study of the periods of the Persian Empire and other world civilizations, such as Lumen Learning Courses in Natural History, see Lumen.

Chapter 10

[55]Cyrus the Great, as quoted in Herodotus (*Cyrus*) 119.

[56]See Frye.

[57]Olmstead 56-58.

[58]See United Nations.

[59]Daniel 1:21, 6:28, 10:1; 2 Chronicles 36:22-23; see also Ezra 1 and Isaiah 44 and 45.

[60]Josephus Book XI:2.

[61]Among many of the articles I have read, I found the recent dissertation of S.D. Anderson to be very insightful as he presses through the many complex issues streams of thought.

[62]Mehta & Endelman.

[63]To learn more, see Mark Bradley's book documenting the realities faced by many Christians living in Iran.

Chapter 11

64 R.C. shared this point as we were in a conversation about themes of this chapter; see   Isaiah 44:6; Revelation 1:8,17;21:6; 22:13.

65"Alpha and Omega."

66See my explanation in Chapter 9.

67"Eschatological" refers to things relating to the end-time plan of God.

68See John 15.

69Daniel 11:1; 5:30-6:1-28.

70Gabriel only appeared in the Bible as it relates to the coming of the Messiah. The next time he appeared was to Zechariah and to Mary to announce the miracle of incarnation. Luke 1:19, 26.

71See Ephesians 2:2; 6:12; Colossians 2:8; 1 Peter 5:8; 2 Corinthians 10:4-5.

72The term "10/40 window" represents a rectangular area on the globe between 10 and 40 degrees north latitude. It is often called "The Resistant Belt" and includes the most unreached people groups and the majority of the world's Muslims, Hindus and Buddhists.

73Huntzinger 45.

Chapter 12

74Henry (*Concise*) 681.

[75]Robinson 42.

[76]Olmstead, p.68-85.

[77]See Matthew 6:33.

[78]See Ezra 7-8; Nehemia 1-2.

Chapter 13

[79]Haman, the son of Hammedatha the Agagite. He is most likely, a descendant of Agag, the king of the Amelkites. God had told king Saul to kill the Amelkites because of the way they treated Israel on their way out of Egypt. Saul did, but failed to kill Agag, who Samuel later killed. It's possible that Haman's hatred of the Jews was due to this family history. Now that he was in power he had the chance to finally revenge. see 1 Samuel 15.

[80]I discuss this further in Chapter 15.

Section 4

[81]See Daniel 2:36-45; 8:20-22.

Chapter 14

[82] Malachi 3:1, 4:4-6, Isaiah 40:1,2.

[83]In the Christian calendar there is an annual holiday, celebrated around the world, known as Epiphany or "Three Kings Day." Epiphany remembers the "revealing" of the Christ to the Gentile world, represented in the arrival of the Persian Magi, who came bearing precious gifts to honour the birth of the King of kings.

[84]One of the fruits of his glory in Egypt is that Egypt later became a key for preserving the theology of the church as well as a centre for world evangelism.

[85]Egypt not only preserved Jesus as a refugee after his birth, but early christian theology flourished and was preserved there. In the history of the early church, many heresies arose. One of the strongest and most dangerous was known as the Arian heresy (named after an Alexandrian priest). This heresy, denying the true divinity of Christ, maintained that the Son was not eternal, nor of one nature with God, but was a dependent instrument, created for the redemption of the world. The bishops of Egypt condemned this and General Council of Nicaea (325) under Athanasius, bishop of Alexandria (296–373), defined and affirmed the doctrine of the coeternity and coequality of God the Father and God the Son. See more on Athanasius, Bishop of Alexandria.

[86]These new believers returned to their nations and shared their faith. For centuries, Egyptian christians have influenced many nations through their writings and testimonies. See Dessert Fathers, Saint Maurice, Saint Samaan.

Chapter 15

[87]In Nazi Germany, many who were against the agenda of Jewish annihilation stood in the gap, not only in prayer, but by risking their lives to loving their neighbors by providing for and hiding Jewish people in their homes. Many were arrested, suffered and died with their Jewish guests. But some, like Corrie Ten Boom survived to tell us their story.

[88]I will not exhaust the scriptures nor the theological view points available, but I hope my journey encourages you to study out (perhaps revisit) scriptures that you may not be familiar with or that you have previously dismissed.

[89]The Day of the Lord is introduced throughout Old Testament prophecy; this descriptive phrase is specifically found in Joel 2:11.

[90]Bickle 1.

Conclusion

[91]See Revelation 19:7; Daniel 11:35; 12:10.

[92]See Matthew 24:42-43; 25:13; Luke 12:38-39; 21:36; 1 Thessalonians 5:2-4, 6; Revelation 3:3; 16:15.

[93]See Revelation 18:20; 19:17-21, 20:4-6, 19:8.

[94]"They have seen Your procession, O God,The procession of my God, my King, into the sanctuary. The singers went before, the players on instruments followed after. Among them were the maidens playing timbrels" Psalm 68:24,25.

SHADI

Sources

(Internet sources accessed in 2023 unless otherwise noted.)

"Alpha and Omega." New World Encyclopedia. June 2023, https://www.newworldEncyclopedia.org/p/index.php?title=AlphaandOmega&oldid=1052779.

Anderson, Steven D. *Darius the Mede: A Reappraisal (A revision of the author's Ph.D.* dissertation from Dallas Theological Seminary, 2014). Grand Rapids: Steven D. Anderson, 2014. www.bible.truthonly.com/darius-the-mede.

Andrews, E. D. *The Bible as History: Medo-Persia, the Fourth World Power of the Bible.* Christian Publishing House Blog, April 2019, https://christianpublishinghouse.co/2019/04/11/the-bible-as-history-medo-persia-the-fourth-world-power-of-the-bible/.

Arnold, Bill T. and Williamson, H.G.M. *Dictionary of the Old Testament: Historical Books.* IVP, 2005.

"Belshazzar." *Encyclopedia Britannica*, 17 Oct. 2008, https://www.britannica.com/biography/Belshazzar.

Bickle, Mike. "Israel, Egypt, and Arabs: Epicenter of God's End-Time Plan." *International House of Prayer University, Forerunner Study Groups:* IHOPU, 11 June 2021, https://mikebickle.org/wp-content/uploads/2021/06/Israel-Egypt-and-Arabs-Epicenter-of-Gods-End-Time-Plan-Isa.-19.24-KD.pdf.

Boutflower, C. *In and Around the Book of Daniel*. The Macmillan Co.,1923. *Internet Archive*, https://archive.org/details/inaroundbookofda00bout/page/n3/mode/2up?q=boutflower.

Bradley, Mark. *Too Many to Jail: The Story of Iran's New Christians*. Monarch Books, 2014.

Bradshaw, Robert. *The Babylonian Exile of Israel*. Archived at https://biblicalstudies.org.uk/article_exile.html.

Brown, Phillip A. *A Literary and Theological Analysis of the Book fo Ezra,* 2004. Archived at Bible.org, https://bible.org/seriespage/introduction-literary-and-theological-analysis-book-ezra.

"Cambyses." *Encyclopedia of the Bible*. Derived from the Zondervan Pictoral Encyclopedia of the Bible, Vols. 1-5, Merril C. Tenney, editor. *BibleGateway*, https://www.biblegateway.com/resources/Encyclopedia-of-the-bible/Cambyses.

Carr, D. M. *An Introduction to the Old Testament: Sacred Texts and Imperial Contexts of the Hebrew Bible*. John Wiley & Sons, 2010.

Coffman, James Burton. "Commentary on Ezra 7." *Coffman's Commentaries on the Bible*. Abilene Christian University Press, 1983-1999. *Studylight*, https://www.studylight.org/commentaries/eng/bcc/ezra-7.html.

Constable, Thomas L. "Notes on Daniel" *Expository Notes on Bible, ed. 2023*. Archived at https://

www.planobiblechapel.org/tcon/notes/html/ot/
daniel/daniel.htm.

---. "Notes on Ezra" *Expository Notes on Bible, ed. 2023*.
Archived at https://www.planobiblechapel.org/
tcon/notes/html/ot/ezra/ezra.htm.

Cooper, Julien."The Earliest Mention of the Place-name
Sinai: The Journeys of Khety." *The Ancient Near
East Today: Journal of the American Society of
Overseas Research*, Vol.11 No.12, Feb. 2023,
https://www.asor.org/anetoday/2023/02/sinai-
journeys-khety/.

"Cyrus Cylinder." *The British Museum*. https://
www.britishmuseum.org/collection/object/
W_1880-0617-1941.

Frye, Richard N. "Cyrus the Great". *Encyclopedia
Britannica*, 8 May 2023, https://
www.britannica.com/biography/Cyrus-the-Great.

Gurney, R. J. "The Four Kingdoms of Daniel 2 and 7."
Themelios, an International Journal for Pastors
and Students of Theological and Religious
Studies, vol.2(Is.2), 39–45, 1977, http://tgc-
documents.s3.amazonaws.com/themelios/
Themelios2.2.pdf.

Henry, M. "Commentary on Daniel 8." *Blue Letter Bible,*
https://www.blueletterbible.org/Comm/mhc/Dan/
Dan*008.cfm*

---. *Concise Commentary on the Bible, 1706.* Archived by
Christian Classics Ethereal Library, 2006, https://

storage.snappages.site/7STCWP/assets/files/
matthew-henrys-bible-commentary.pdf.

Herodotus. *The Histories, Book I: Chapters 189-192* (5th
Century). Online publication of the *Loeb Classical
Library Edition*, 1920, in the Public Domain,
https://penelope.uchicago.edu/Thayer/E/Roman/
Texts/Herodotus/1D*.html.

House, Paul R. and Eric Mitchell. *Old Testament Survey,
2nd ed.* B&H Publishing   Group, 2007.

Huntzinger, Allyn. *Persians in the Bible*. Persian World
Outreach, 2007.

Josephus, Flavius. *Antiquities of the Jews, Book XI:2.*
https://penelope.uchicago.edu/josephus/
ant-11.html.

Mehta, C., & Endelman, G. "How Cyrus' View of Religious
Toleration May Have Inspired the American
Constitution." *The Insightful Immigration Blog*, Mar.
2016, blog.cyrusmehta.com/2013/07/how-cyrus-
view-of-religious-toleration-may-have-inspired-the-
american-constitution.html#.

Nijssen, Daan. "Cyrus the Great." *World History
Encyclopedia,* July 2022, www.worldhistory.org/
Cyrus_the_Great.

Olmstead, A.T. *History of the Persian Empire*, University of
Chicago Press, 1948. *Institute for the Study of
Ancient Cultures*, https://isac.uchicago.edu/
research/publications/misc/history-persian-
Empire.

Richardson, Joel. *Mount Sinai in Arabia: The True Location Revealed*. Winepress, 2019.

Robinson, Theodore H. *A History of Israel, Vol.II*. Oxford Clarendon Press, 1932. *Internet Archive*, https://archive.org/details/historyofisrael0002robi_p1r6/page/42/mode/1up.

Shurpin, Yehuda. "How Was Jacob Embalmed?" *Chabad.Org*, 2023, www.chabad.org/library/article*cdo/aid/5337988/jewish/How-Was-Jacob-Embalmed-Is-It-Against-Torah*.htm.

Lumen."The Persian Empire - World Civilizations 1 (HIS101) - Biel." *Lumen Learning Open Education Resource*, https://courses.lumenlearning.com/suny-fmcc-boundless-worldhistory/chapter/the-persian-Empire/.

Storms, Sam. "Introduction to Daniel." *Sam Storms - Enjoying God,* https://www.samstorms.org/all-articles/post/introduction-to-daniel.

United Nations. "Universal Declaration of Human Rights, 1948*." United Nations,* https://www.un.org/en/about-us/universal-declaration-of-human-rights.

Xenophon. *Xenophon's Cyrus the Great: The Arts of Leadership and War,* edited by Larry Hedrick, Truman Talley Books, 2006.

"Zedekiah." *Encyclopedia Britannica*, 12 May 2014, https://www.britannica.com/biography/Zedekiah.

SHADI

About the Author

Shadi was born and raised in the Middle East. Having carried a strong conviction since his childhood to serve the Lord full-time, he left his career as a medical doctor to pursue this passion. He has served in international ministry contexts for more than twenty-five years, mobilising prayer within and for the nations and people of the Middle East. One of his great joys, apart from fathering his own children, is seeing young people equipped and commissioned to accomplish all that God has destined for their lives. He and his wife, together with their children, are serving the Lord in the nations.

About PublishU

PublishU is transforming the world of publishing.

PublishU has developed a new and unique approach to publishing books, offering a three-step guided journey to becoming a globally published author!

We enable hundreds of people a year to write their book within 100-days, publish their book in 100-days and launch their book over 100-days to impact tens of thousands of people worldwide.

The journey is transformative, one author said,

"I never thought I would be able to write a book, let alone in 100 days... now I'm asking myself what else have I told myself that can't be done that actually can?'"

To find out more visit
www.PublishU.com

SHADI

Printed by Amazon Italia Logistica S.r.l.
Torrazza Piemonte (TO), Italy

65649124R00131